KU-178-858

Thomas Cook

CITYSPOTS
BILBAO

Patrick McConnell

Written by Patrick McConnell
Updated by Iratxe Ormatza Imatz

Published by Thomas Cook Publishing
A division of Thomas Cook Tour Operations Limited
Company registration No: 1450464 England
The Thomas Cook Business Park, 9 Coningsby Road
Peterborough PE3 8SB, United Kingdom
Email: sales@thomascook.com, Tel: +44 (0)1733 416477
www.thomascookpublishing.com

Produced by The Content Works Ltd
Aston Court, Kingsmead Business Park, Frederick Place
High Wycombe, Bucks HP11 1LA
www.thecontentworks.com

Series design based on an original concept by Studio 183 Limited

ISBN: 978-1-84157-869-9

First edition © 2006 Thomas Cook Publishing
This second edition © 2008 Thomas Cook Publishing
Text © Thomas Cook Publishing
Maps © Thomas Cook Publishing/PCGraphics (UK) Limited
Transport map © Communicarta Limited

Series Editor: Kelly Anne Pipes
Production/DTP: Steven Collins

Printed and bound in Spain by GraphyCems

Cover photography (Guggenheim Museum) © Gräfenhain Günter/4Corners Images

CONTENTS

SYMBOLS KEY

The following symbols are used throughout this book:

ⓐ address ☏ telephone ⓕ fax ⓦ website address ⓔ email
🕒 opening times ⓝ public transport connections

The following symbols are used on the maps:

🛈	information office	▨	points of interest
🛫	airport	◯	city
➕	hospital	○	large town
🛡	police station	○	small town
🚌	bus station	=	motorway
🚆	railway station	—	main road
Ⓜ	metro		minor road
✝	cathedral	—	railway
❶	numbers denote featured cafés & restaurants		

Hotels and restaurants are graded by approximate price as follows:
£ budget price ££ mid-range price £££ expensive

Abbreviations used in addresses:
C/ (Calle)
Pl. (Plaza)
Av. (Avenida)

◗ *The Guggenheim Museum has become the icon of modern Bilbao*

Introduction

The city of Bilbao, proud bastion of the Basque way of life, is witnessing a major cultural renaissance. It has much to offer the discerning traveller: history, art, architecture, fine cuisine, lifestyle, shopping, and easy access to fishing villages, beaches and natural parks. The construction of the famous Guggenheim Museum, among other regeneration projects, lifted the city's image into the top rank of European cities. Set within the Mar Cantábrico, or Bay of Biscay, Spain's fourth-largest city has risen to the challenge of overcoming its legacy of industrialisation and pollution – so much so that it has become a model of regeneration for other cities.

The reasons for visiting this Basque city and its countryside are as varied as they are plentiful. The city's top cultural establishments, the foremost being of course the Guggenheim, are considered European highlights, and the newer, dynamic areas like the Ensanche provide a contrast to the atmospheric historic centre, with its web of ancient streets.

Bilbao is also a handy base for visits to the countryside and natural parks, and provides easy access to the seaside town of San Sebastián, justly considered one of Spain's loveliest places, and quiet, charming Vitoria, seat of the Basque government. The magnificent coastline of the Costa Vasca offers rewards for those who venture out of Bilbao, with fishing villages like Hondarriba and Elantxobe, and beautiful bays such as Bahía de la Concha. In addition, the Bay of Biscay offers numerous fine beaches, from the resort of Getxo along the coast to Lekeiteo and beyond.

The Basque country, Euskadi to its natives, remains an unspoiled region, despite the historical development of industry on the peninsula. Rural traditions are well preserved and are an important element of the Basque life. The economic recession has been arrested by major urban renewal and the pollution of the Rio Nervión is now taken more seriously. The airport and metro gave the city a fresh start with this regeneration. Bilbao is increasingly popular with visitors and the word is out, so get in and explore it while it's fresh.

🔺 *Bilbao cathedral's spire above the streets of Casco Viejo*

When to go

SEASONS & CLIMATE

Sitting on Spain's north coast, on the Bay of Biscay, Bilbao has an Atlantic climate, so you will need to be prepared for rain. The Atlantic seaboard regions are sometimes called Green Spain, owing to the amount of rain they receive. Bilbao and these regions are well known for their wet weather, as celebrated most famously by the Spanish poet Federico García Lorca in his Galician poems. Showers should therefore be expected at any time of the year, even in summer. Luckily, there's a lot to do and see in Bilbao even when the weather is inclement (see page 52–3). The area does not get as hot as it does further south in Spain and there are cooler breezes to be found, particularly on higher ground. However, the Basque coast does still get plenty of sun; it is, after all, on the same latitude as Perpignan in the south of France. You'll need to protect yourself against sunburn and cover up exposed skin if you're visiting in summer.

January–February is cool, with maximum temperatures of 9–10°C (48–50°F). Spring weather (March–May) is unsettled, with marked variations of cold and warmth: the average temperature can vary between 11° and 16°C (52–60°F). True summer begins in June, and until the end of July you can count on dry, warm weather, averaging 21°C (70°F). August, though still as warm, brings with it the possibility of thunderstorms and the rainy season gets going in September. October is cooler, but still a very pleasant 16°C (60°F), and this is one of the best months in which to visit; by November the temperature usually drops sharply as the wet Basque winter gets under way.

The emergence of no-frills airlines has made Bilbao much more accessible for short breaks from Britain. However, the seasonal fare variations are wide and fares differ sharply also according to the day of the week you choose for your outward and return flight. It pays to investigate thoroughly before choosing dates.

ANNUAL EVENTS

Bilbao and its surrounding areas host a rich variety of traditional festivals. No matter when you visit you are bound to come across a major or minor celebration.

Fireworks feature in many of the Spanish festivals and the Basques are happy to oblige with superb displays of their own.

January

La Tamborrada, San Sebastián (20 January) This 24-hour drumming extravaganza sees troupes of uniformed drummers parade through the streets of San Sebastián in high-volume celebration.

February

Procession of San Blas (3 February) San Blas, the Christian martyr famed for feats of miraculous healing, is honoured by a procession through the streets of Bilbao. Stalls selling doughnuts and the coloured cords of San Blas are set up in the Plaza del Arenal. Traditionally, the faithful wear cords around the neck for nine days, having had them blessed in the church of San Nicolás in the plaza, and then burn them; this is said to give protection from throat infections for a year.

Santa Águeda (4 February) Choirs in traditional dress take to the streets to sing songs about Santa Águeda, marking time with a staff.

● *Grotesque 'giants', a feature of festivals across the region*

Carnival The approach of Lent is the occasion for Carnival, a huge event all over Spain. Bilbao, Vitoria and San Sebastián all have their own carnivals, which involve street processions and cavalcades.

March–April
Easter Semana Santa or Easter Week sees street processions in Bilbao, which begin at the church of Santos Juanes in the Casco Viejo. Revered relics such as the Cristo de la Villa, dating from 1590, are carried around the town. On Easter Sunday the Basques celebrate their national holiday or Aberri Aguna.

May–June
Arrain Azoka (third weekend of May) This festival is devoted to fish and seafood and takes place in the fishing village of Bermeo.
Eve of San Juan (24 June) This pagan bonfire festival is held all around Spain, and in Bilbao it is held at Artxanda.
Summer festivals From June throughout the summer there are numerous festivals in small towns and traditional sport shows.

July
Getxo Jazz Festival This major jazz fest opens the Jazz Festival series in the Basque Country (others are held in Vitoria, San Sebastián and Bayonne). Some concerts are free, but tickets for the star performances

SMALL TOWN FIESTAS
These summer fiestas are pagan by tradition but nowadays they are a celebration of the town's saint. During the day there are Basque traditional sports, food competitions, games for kids, and at night bonfires and music. Some of the best are Elantxobe, 29 June; Gernika, 15–18 August; Gorliz, 25 July; Lekeitio, 28 June– 1 July and 2–6 September; and Bermeo, 7–16 September. For more information, contact the tourist office in Bilbao ☏ 944 795 760

and group competition cost €10–25. ☎ 944 319 280
✉ info@getxokultura.com 🌐 www.getxo.net

International Folklore Festival Takes place in Portugalete, and brings
in folk dancing companies from around the world.

Jazzaldia (last week July) San Sebastián hosts one of the most
important jazz festivals in Europe, with outdoor and indoor
concerts. ☎ 943 481 900 🌐 www.jazzaldia.com
✉ jazzaldia@donostia.org

Bilboko Kalealdia This street theatre and arts festival takes place
after the Gexto Jazz Festival and fills Bilbao's streets and squares
for six evenings with dance, theatre and circus performances
and processions.

August

Aste Nagusia/Semana Grande (Big Week) On 15 August, for the
Feast of the Virgin of Begoña, crowds of the faithful converge on
the Basílica de Nuestra Señora de Begoña, east of the old town.
From the Saturday following the 15th, citizens celebrate Aste Nagusia,
otherwise known as Semana Grande. This is Bilbao's biggest festival,
a time for firework displays and street parties, street theatre, and
free outdoor pop and rock concerts. During Semana Grande, many
bilbaínos, as locals are known, gather in *konparsas*, which are cultural
and social clubs that organise gastronomy, sports competitions,
concerts and theatre at the stands that are set up for the week.
Festivals also take place in Vitoria and San Sebastián. ☎ 944 795 760
🌐 www.bilbao.net/bilbaoturismo

September

San Sebastián International Film Festival ☎ 943 481 212
🌐 www.sansebastianfestival.com

🔺 *You can see all kinds of Basque sports played at festival time*

Boat Races (first and second Sunday in September) This major Basque rowing competition, a tradition since 1879, sees eight teams of 13 compete over a three-mile course. It takes place at the Bahía de la Concha. Ⓦ www.donostiasansebastian.com

⬥ *Parades of giants are a colourful feature of the Aste Nagusia celebrations*

NATIONAL PUBLIC HOLIDAYS
New Year's Day 1 Jan
Saint Joseph 19 Mar
Easter 20–24 Mar 2008, 9–13 Apr 2009
Labour Day 1 May
St James' Day 25 July
Assumption 15 Aug
Spanish National Day 12 Oct
All Saints' Day 1 Nov
Constitution Day 6 Dec
Immaculate Conception 8 Dec
Christmas Day 25 Dec

October–December
Contemporary Dance and Theatre Festival Innovative dance and
theatre performances take place at La Fundición, Arriaga, Bilborock,
Bilbaoescena, CDM San Francisco and Merced Ikastetxea.
🅦 www.badbilbao.com
International Festival of Documentary and Short Film Screenings at
theatres and cinemas, and also free screenings for up to 30 people
in Plaza Arriaga outside the Arriaga Theatre. 🅐 Colón de Larreategui
37 🅣 944 248 698 🅦 www.zinebi.com
Festival of Santo Tomás (21 December) Locals buy fresh produce in
time for Christmas at hundreds of stalls selling fresh fruit, vegetables
and turkey, which are set up between Plaza del Arenal and Plaza Nueva
in the old town. Shoppers take their refreshment at the many booths
selling savoury cooked sausages inside a *talo*, a kind of taco, and
glasses of *txakoli* (see page 130).

Basque Country

Euskal Herria is the name Basque people give to their land, referring to the three provinces that make up the Basque autonomous community: Gipuzkoa, Bizkaia and Alava. There are another four provinces, one on the Spanish side – Navarra, whose capital is Pamplona – and another three on the French side, over the Pyrenees. The Basque language unifies the seven provinces.

The origins of the Basques remain uncertain but the archaeological evidence suggests that they have inhabited the western part of the Pyrenees for thousands of years. Finds date back to as early as the Palaeolithic era, around 9000 BC. Basque people have been described as the last survivors of Europe's original population. Their language, Euskara, stretches back into antiquity and is apparently not related to any other European language. The themes of distinctive Basque pre-Christian myths and legends featuring giants and demons predominate in much of the traditional culture of this region. The Basques absorbed Christianity, at the same time building on their old beliefs to maintain devout religious traditions.

At the outset of the Spanish Civil War in the 1930s, the industrial centres of Bizkaia and Gipuzkoa supported the Republican cause, while the conservative Navarrans and Arabans in neighbouring rural areas joined the Nationalists. An autonomous Basque government was declared in 1936 but the Basques suffered heavily under Franco, starting with the bombing of the city of Gernika by German forces in April 1937. This is often cited as the first civilian target in the history of aerial bombing. Franco's Nationalists made the Basques pay a heavy price for declaring autonomy, killing over 21,000 people. The poet and philosopher Miguel de Unamuno (1864–1937) famously rejected fascism in the face of Nationalist sympathisers and died under house arrest. Although very much a Basque and proud of it, he criticised myth-making about the Basque people and their origins. He spoke out both in support of what he thought was right and to criticise dictators such as Primo de Rivera. It is hard to imagine him tolerating the brutal regime of Franco had he lived on.

With the Nationalist forces' victory, a centralist right-wing administration was imposed on the whole of Spain under Franco's rule; it had little time for regional autonomy and the Basques were repressed. Their language was banned and central government was imposed by force from the outside. Unsurprisingly, this led to a mass exodus of Basques into France and J. A. Aguirre's Basque government exiled to Paris. There were difficult times for exiled Basques ahead, particularly with the onset of World War II and the rise of the unsympathetic French Vichy regime.

Basque nationalism has always been fiercely defended throughout its turbulent history. The rise of a more militant Basque version in the shape of ETA (Euskadi ta Askatasuna, 'Basque Homeland and Freedom') earned the region notoriety from the 1960s onwards through a campaign of bombings and assassinations, which did not stop with the restoration of democracy in Spain. Alongside this, however, has been the growth of more peaceful politics, with a move away from the tactics of terrorism by ETA; there was a ceasefire between 1998 and 1999, and in March 2006 a ceasefire was declared, but has since been forsaken. The Basque language is once again taught and the Basque flag flies all over the region. The return to democracy in Spain and the new constitution has given limited autonomy to the Basques, their own Parliament and right to collect taxes.

History

The Basque people were already well established in this region when the Romans arrived in the 1st century BC; the Romans prudently recognised the independence of the tribes of the Vascones, as they called them, with an agreement on passage and trade, and the Basques were left pretty much to their own devices. In the Dark Ages the Visigoths, Germanic tribes who conquered most of post-Roman Spain, tried to vanquish the Basque peoples but they proved very difficult to overcome, something that numerous invaders found over the centuries. The Moors conquered as far north as Pamplona but never overthrew the people of the Euskal Herria. The Basques united in 818 to form the Kingdom of Navarra. They adopted Christianity but kept their own traditions and customs, such as the *fueros*, the ancient laws under which they governed themselves.

Bilbao was founded in 1300 by Diego López de Haro, a lord from Vizcaya. The early city economy was primarily based on fishing and later on industry. By 1512 the kings of a united Spain gained control of the Basque region in return for granting it self-government. This state of autonomy continued for the next two centuries, with Philip V granting the Basques the right to trade with the newly discovered Americas. In the same year, the Spanish Duke of Alba divided Navarra in two: south and north, with the latter falling on the French side.

Napoleon respected their *fueros* in the constitution he drew up for Spain, in return for their support. Later in the 19th century the Carlist Wars broke out between the liberals and conservatives. Most Basques fought along with the conservatives, as the king Charles V promised he would respect the *fueros*. This acted as a catalyst for the growth of Basque nationalism in the 19th century and the Basque Nationalist party was established in 1895.

By the mid-19th century Bilbao had become a major centre of industry, based on the region's mineral deposits. During the Spanish Civil War it was one of the industrial centres that declared support for the Republicans and paid a heavy price after the Spanish Nationalist forces' victory, with repression of all signs of autonomy and Basque culture. In response, the ETA movement began a long campaign of assassinations and bombings, often killing or wounding politicians or policemen, but sometimes targeting the Spanish tourist industry.

However, there has been a change since the late 1990s. With the development of the Basque Parliament came the rise of more peaceful politics, and the Lizarra-Garazi agreement. Nevertheless, the constitution of Spain, based on the unity of the state, is still rejected by many Basque Nationalists. There was a ceasefire between 1998 and 1999, and then again from March 2006 to June 2007.

Bilbao was badly hit by the collapse of traditional industry in the 1980s and 1990s. This did, however, lead to the emergence of a prosperous, modern city, which has dealt positively with its urban sprawl and industrial legacy. Much unspoiled land remains, especially outside the urban areas. The building of the Guggenheim Museum has led the way in the regeneration of this ancient seaport and its new lease of life as a tourist destination, a process now called the 'Guggenheim effect' and much envied by cities around the world in a similar situation.

Lifestyle

The Basque lifestyle is very different from that of the typical North European. Many writers and visitors have commented on the slower pace of life. There is a greater emphasis on social time in cafés and bars and talking to friends, especially on Thursday and Friday nights, and at weekends. The family is held in high esteem as a social institution, and its importance in Basque life would be difficult to overestimate.

Eating is an art in itself in Bilbao, and there are plenty of opportunities to tuck in: cakes and croissants for breakfast, *pintxos* (Basque tapas) to get you through until lunch, three courses for

lunch, a small cake in the afternoon or *pintxos* in the evening, and meat, fresh fish and seafood for dinner. In the evening there are late meals that extend far into the night, as the Basques like to take their time eating and relaxing with family and friends.

It is still traditional to take siestas, even if the heat is less intense here than in the south. Many shops and offices close for a couple of hours at lunchtime and don't open till later on in the afternoon. However, this way of life is now seen as changing, due in part to pressure from the 'North European' model.

The café is at the centre of Bilbao's gregarious, outdoor lifestyle

Culture

So much of culture in Bilbao and its neighbouring areas is bound up in the Basque identity, and the language of the Basques, Euskera, is at the heart of that identity. The first book in Euskera was a collection of poems by Bernart Etxepare in 1545. The decline of the Basque language has been halted in part thanks to the introduction of Basque in schools and the growing awareness among people about the need to speak it to preserve it.

Basque bards remain popular to this day, and poem improvisers – the traditional Basque version of rappers – are also held in high esteem. Basque music is distinctive, with musicians playing traditional musical instruments (including the *txistu*, a traditional small flute, the wind instrument *alboka* and the *txalaparta*, on which two people play with wood sticks) to perform pieces written as far back as the 16th century. Basques love singing and do so with passion. Traditional dances still feature in the villages, especially at fiestas. Some of these can be very lively and even warlike, others more social, in elaborate dress and with fancy steps.

The city of Bilbao has seen a remarkable cultural resurgence. This is reflected in the existence of some splendid museums, galleries and performance centres that are to be found in Bilbao and its neighbouring towns. Cultural highlights include:

Guggenheim Museum (see pages 88–91) The Guggenheim almost single-handedly put Bilbao on the cultural tourist map. Although there is much more to the city than this one museum, it remains the

● *The Guggenheim shouldn't be missed, but be prepared for queues at peak times*

must-see attraction, both for its architecture and for the artistic riches it contains.

Museo de Bellas Artes (Fine Arts Museum) (see pages 91–3) Counterbalancing the modernity of the Guggenheim, this more traditional art gallery has many treasures by Basque, Spanish and international artists.

Meseo Maritimo (Maritime Museum) (see pages 93–4) This new museum in the old dockyards, commemorating Bilbao's long association with seafaring, is well worth a visit.

Museo Vasco (see pages 71–2) This museum in the old town has a very mixed collection on the theme of all things Basque, and is a great way to get an understanding of Basque culture through the centuries.

Teatro Arriaga (see page 72) Not only an architectural jewel inside and out, this neo-baroque theatre is a venue for performances of opera, dance and drama.

Bridges The many bridges over the Río Nervión are worth an itinerary of their own, demonstrating the art of bridge building from medieval times (those connecting the old town with new Bilbao), through the 19th century (the engineering tour de force of the Puente Colgante; see pages 86–8) to graceful modern structures such as the Puente Zubizuri (see page 84).

◗ *Basque sculptor Oteiza's masterpiece opposite the Town Hall*

Shopping

WHERE TO SHOP

Bilbao affords plenty of opportunities for shopping. The two main shopping areas are the Gran Vía, a broad pedestrianised street that runs across the north of modern Bilbao from the Plaza Circular to the Plaza del Sagrado Corazón, and the Casco Viejo (or old centre).

Some of Bilbao's finest shops and department stores are located on the Gran Vía, and in the section between Plaza Moyúa and Plaza Circular and around. You will find Basque designer Ion Fiz's shop, local chain stores such as clothing store For (ⓦ www.for.es) and big chains such as Mango, Custo and El Corte Inglés. The latter is a branch of Spain's best-known department store chain, offering a huge range of merchandise, from fashion, books and cosmetics to household and sporting goods.

The Casco Viejo has always been a shopping area and many of its streets, such as Calle Sombrerería (milliners' street), still carry the names of the trades in which they specialised. The area still has many independent, traditional shops (particularly shoe shops), as well as new young designers and chain stores. The main shopping streets of the old centre include the Siete Calles (see page 71), Calle Bidebarrieta and Calle Correo.

The most central shopping mall is **Zubiarte** (ⓐ Lehendakari Leizaola 2 ❶ 944 277 380 ⓦ www.zubiarte.com ● 10.00–22.00 Ⓜ Metro: Abandoibarra), next to the Puente de Deusto, with more than 70 shops, a supermarket, a cinema and numerous cafés and restaurants.

Be warned that shops in the centre of Bilbao are closed on Sundays, with the exception of some bakeries and newsagents.

◆ Gran Via is lined with boutiques and stores of all kinds

USEFUL SHOPPING PHRASES

What time do the shops open/close?
¿A qué hora abren/cierran las tiendas?
¿A kay ora abren/theeyerran las teeyendas?

How much is this?
¿Cuánto es?
¿Cwantoe es?

Can I try this on?
¿Puedo probarme esto?
¿Pwedo probarme esto?

My size is ...
Mi número es el ...
Mee noomero es el ...

I'll take this one, thank you
Me llevo éste
Meh llievo esteh

This is too large/too small/too expensive.
Do you have any others?
Es muy grande/muy pequeño/muy caro. ¿Tienen más?
Es mooy grandeh/mooy pekenio/mooy karo. ¿Teeyenen mas?

It's not only the small ones that are closed – even big shopping centres on the edge of town shut all day on Sundays.

MARKETS
Market day is typically the main weekly event of many towns and villages in the region, and markets take place every day of the week in Bilbao. Mercado de la Ribera is a huge covered market where you can find plenty of fresh fruit and vegetables, and from time to time it holds cultural events.

WHAT TO BUY

Gifts and souvenirs can be bought all over the city, including at the shops of the galleries and museums, such as the Guggenheim and the Fine Arts Museum. Basque specialities include wood carving, weaving and other handicrafts. Fine local food and wines are also good buys. The best areas are the Casco Viejo and around the Guggenheim for handicrafts and souvenirs, and the Mercado de la Ribera for fresh food. Fashion boutiques, ranging from international designer outlets such as MaxMara to small independents, can be found throughout the city, but particularly around Gran Vía. Leatherwear of all kinds is good value.

○ *Fish at Bilbao's market*

Eating & drinking

Traditional Basque dishes are famous around the world, and for good reason. Because of the region's proximity to the sea, fish and seafood are an important part of Basque cuisine. The riches of the countryside can also be found in tasty meat dishes, along with local vegetables (locally grown red pepper is a key ingredient). *Marmitako* is a fish stew and *bacalao* dishes are based on cod, cooked in a variety of ways, such as *bacalao al pil-pil* (cooked with garlic) or *a la bizkaina* (cooked with dried red peppers). Fish soup is another good option. Tuna and cod feature regularly, as does *merluza* (or hake). Tuna is frequently cooked in spices, garlic, tomatoes and aubergines, and *merluza a la koskera*, (hake served in a white wine sauce) is a very popular dish in Bilbao. *Txipirones* is baby squid in its own ink or grilled with onions, and elvers (baby eels) are an exquisite (and very expensive) delicacy eaten around Christmas time.

Meat dishes include grilled or oven-cooked lamb chops and T-bone beef steak is served almost raw, eaten on its own and accompanied by a good Rioja wine or cider. Chorizo is a spicy sausage that is often combined with other dishes. Flat corn cakes, or *talos*, were traditionally eaten like bread; these days they often feature in winter festivals such as Santo Tomás, and can be either savoury or sweet.

The new Basque cuisine, or *nueva cocina vasca*, uses typical Basque staples to create exciting new dishes. Think wild mushrooms, crêpes with spider crabs or sea bass with green pepper.

There are plenty of local tipples, with grapes and apples forming the basis of what is on offer. Wine is the most famous local beverage. Rioja, made on the edge of the Basque region, is the region's best-known red, made mainly with tempranillo grapes, along with

> **PRICE CATEGORIES**
> The restaurant price guides used in the book are based on the
> average price of a two-course dinner for one without drinks.
> **£** up to €25 **££** €25–€50 **£££** above €50

Navarra clarets. Local *txakoli* is a light fruity drink, with a touch of
acidity. *Sidra* (cider) is a local speciality, especially in the countryside.
Anis is popular and is sometimes mixed with other drinks, such as
cognac, which is also used to flavour coffee (known as *carajillo*).
Patxaran is a very popular liqueur made with anis and sloes,
which many families still make at home.

No-one should leave Bilbao without having spent at least
one evening drifting from bar to bar eating tapas, known here as
pintxos. The city has a wide range of cafés and *tabernas* (pubs or
bars). Though the modern part of Bilbao doesn't lack good places
to eat and drink, the Casco Viejo or old centre, east of the river,
has the richest pickings; try along Calle Santa Maria, the Calle
Barrencalle Barrena or the Plaza Nueva for some of the best
restaurants and *pintxos*.

For the best value when lunching or dining out always look for
the *menú del día*, which is a complete meal of three courses (and
often comes with a bottle of wine) for a single, fixed price, usually
stated outside the restaurant. Wherever you choose to eat, you will
usually find that *la cuenta* (the bill) does not include service, so a tip
is in order if you have been served well.

◆ *A typical street scene in Bilbao's Casco Viejo*

USEFUL DINING PHRASES

I would like a table for ... people
Quisiera una mesa para ... personas
Keyseeyera oona mesa para ... personas

Waiter/waitress!
¡Camarero/Camarera!
¡Camareroe/Camarera!

May I have the bill, please?
¿Podría traerme la cuenta por favor?
¿Pordreea trayerme la cwenta por farbor?

Could I have it well-cooked/medium/rare please?
¿Por favor, la carne bien cocinada/al punto/roja?
¿Por fabor, la kahrrne beeyen kotheeda/al poontoh/roha?

I am a vegetarian. Does this contain meat?
Soy vegetariano. ¿Tiene carne este plato?
Soy begetahreeahnoh. ¿Teeyene carneh esteh plahtoh?

Where is the toilet (restroom) please?
¿Dónde están los servicios, por favor?
¿Donde estan los serbeetheeos, por fabor?

I would like a cup of/two cups of/another coffee/tea
Quisiera una taza de/dos tazas de/otra taza de café/té
Keyseeyera oona tatha dey/dos tathas dey/otra tatha dey kafey/tey

Entertainment & nightlife

The evening is the time to have fun in Bilbao. The city's nightlife comes in all levels of intensity, from an early evening tapas crawl to a late meal, progressing to a disco or club. Dinner is taken later in the evening. A Bilbao night on the town will nearly always begin with some early bar-hopping, and *pintxos* and drinks, at about 19.30. Typically you should wait until 20.00 at the very earliest to think about dinner; the *pintxos* should sustain you until then. If you want to go dancing afterwards try some of the clubs listed on pages 75–9 and 98–100.

BARS & CLUBS

Start the night in the Casco Viejo with some relaxed early bar-hopping, known as *txikiteo*. Enjoy *poteo* (small glasses of wine) or *zurito* (a small beer), accompanied by *pintxos*. The liveliest bars can be found in this area, and the busiest bars are on Calle Pelota, Calle Barrenkale, Calle Somera, Calle Santa Maria, Calle Jardines and Calle Perro. For outdoor *poteo*, pull up a chair at one of the outdoor cafés on lovely Plaza Nueva.

The bars along Calle Ledesma next to Plaza Circular, just across the river in the newer part of town, are popular haunts for an early evening bar crawl. Los Jardines de Albia, particularly the Café Iruña, is also a good spot for cafés, bars and taverns, some of which have live music. Other good bar-hopping areas include Licenciado Poza (very busy on football match Sundays) and around Plaza Indautxu.

MUSIC

You'll have little trouble in finding live music in Bilbao's bars and clubs, but it may pay to do some research before heading out. The local papers have listings and the *Bilbao Guide* from the tourist office (see page 151) should be consulted for up-to-date details. The Palacio Euskalduna (beyond the Guggenheim) stages concerts, and there is a bandstand in El Arenal, beside the church of San Nicolás, where you can hear music. During street festivals, especially 'Big Week' in August (see page 12), there are plenty of free performances around town.

THEATRE

Unless your Spanish or Basque is pretty good, or you are into opera, you may find it difficult to enjoy local performances. The two main venues for performances are:

Teatro Arriaga Opera, theatre and comedy shows.
Pl. Arriaga 1 Information 944 792 036, Tickets 944 310 310
www.teatroarriaga.com Metro: Casco Viejo; Tram: Arriagaa

Palacio Euskalduna de Congresos y de la Música The Palacio's programme features musicals and plays, concerts and conferences
C/Abandoibarra 4 944 035 000 www.euskalduna.net
Metro: San Mamés; Tram: Euskalduna

CINEMA

Multicines (C/Eskuza Metro: San Mamés) and the
Renoir (Lehendakari Agirre Metro: Deusto) offer films in their original language. See local newspapers for more information.

Sport & relaxation

SPECTATOR SPORTS

Football

Fútbol is the most popular sport in Spain and the Basque region is no exception, despite its variety of homegrown sports. Athletic de Bilbao is based at the Estadio de San Mamés and home matches take place on Sundays. They are popular with families, which makes for a friendly atmosphere. The club is almost regarded as the Basque national team, especially when playing against Real Madrid. Tickets are generally easy to get hold of – either from the stadium itself or from one of the BBK ATMs around town with full-size keyboards – with the exception of big games, or those against other Basque teams such as Real Sociedad de San Sebastián.

Athletic de Bilbao Ⓦ www.athletic-club.es Ⓜ Metro: San Mamés; Tram: San Mamés

Pelota

Traditional Basque handball is reputed to be the fastest ball game in the world. Matches can be seen mainly during the summer months, when the championships are held. In Bilbao the game is played both with bare hands or with a bat at the court (*frontón*) at Calle Esperanza 6 (Ⓣ 944 354 740 Ⓜ Metro: Casco Viejo), or you can watch the professionals at **Club Deportivo Bilbao** Ⓐ C/Alameda Rekalde Ⓜ Metro: Moyúa.

Bullfighting

Bullfights are a typical element of many festivals in the Basque Country. Ernest Hemingway famously wrote about the sport but these days it's the subject of much opposition, not only internationally but also within Spain, from the Asociación Defensa Derechos Animal

BULLS AND BULLFIGHTS

Bullfighting is huge in Bilbao and the Basque region, where it is seen as an artistic performance. Bullfights are major events, with teams of *corridas* and *toreros* and then the *matador*. A bullfighting programme lasts about two hours. Bullfights are not easy for visitors to get into; tickets are scarce because of the sport's popularity with locals. Buy tickets at the Plaza de Toros or on-line ⓦ www.plazatorosbilbao.com

Bull running (*encierros*), where spectators become participants and literally run away from charging bulls, takes place most famously in Navarra and in Pamplona at the Festival of Los Sanfermines in July.

As well as at Pamplona, bull running takes place in Tudela (last week of July), Falces (with cows, August), Tafalla (August) and Sanguesa (September).

(ⓦ www.addaong.org). The best toreros can be seen during the Semana Grande (see page 12). The Plaza de Toros de Vista Alegre is south of the city centre; tickets cost between €4 and €120.
Plaza de Toros de Vista Alegre ⓐ C/Martin Agüero ⓣ 944 448 698 ⓛ 10.30–13.00, 16.00–18.00 Mon–Fri ⓜ Metro: Indautxu

PARTICIPATION SPORTS

Bilbao has a number of *polideportivos* (public sports centres). Those in the Artxanda, Deusto, Rekalde, San Ignazio and Txurdinaga districts share an on-line booking system (ⓦ www.bilbaokirolak.com). The entrance fee is roughly €6, and there are additional charges for courts and pitches. If you intend to go more than once, buy a *bono* of five or ten tickets.

Polideportivo de Begoña The largest and best-equipped sports centre in Bilbao, the Begoña sports centre houses two indoor swimming pools, gyms, and squash and tennis courts. It is also a good place to play pelota, traditional Basque handball. ⓐ Circo Amateur del Club Deportivo 2 (Txurdinaga) ⓑ 09.00–21.00 ⓜ Metro: Santutxu

Club Deportivo Bilbao This private club is situated in the heart of the city, just a short distance from the Guggenheim. It has pelota courts, saunas, gyms and swimming pools, and is a stylish place to keep in shape. There's also a barber, TV lounge and restaurant. ⓐ C/Alameda Rekalde 28 ⓣ 944 231 108 ⓦ www.club-deportivo.com ⓑ 07.00–23.00 ⓜ Metro: Moyúa

Golf

There's a golf course in Bilbao (**Real Sociedad Golf Neguri** ⓣ 944 910 200) and San Sebastián (**Golf de Basozabal** ⓣ 943 472 736 ⓜ Metro: Neguri)

Riding

The lovely landscape around Bilbao makes fine territory for horse riding. Riding centres are listed in tourist information offices and brochures.

Adventure sports

A wide range of activities, including canoeing and kayaking, diving, nature walks, surfing and bicycle hire, all based around the Urdaibai Biosphere Reserve (see page 135), is offered by UR 2000, who can also provide instruction. The Bilbao office is in the Casco Viejo.
UR2000 ⓐ Esperanza 26 ⓣ 944 790 656 ⓦ www.ur2000.com ⓜ Metro: Casco Viejo

ⓞ *Doña Casilda park is a peaceful place to walk around*

Accommodation

Accommodation in Bilbao and on the Basque coast as a whole tends to fall in a higher price category than the rest of Spain. The Basque government has introduced an *agroturismo* homestay programme, for which farmers offer bed and breakfast. Local tourist offices here are very helpful and have full listings of what is available in the area.

The best places to stay in the city are mostly located in the old town, the Casco Viejo, many of them along the Calle Bidebarrieta, which runs from Plaza Arriaga down to the cathedral, and in the streets around it, including Calle Lotería, Calle Santa María, Jardines and Calle Maria Muñoz.

In the city centre, the streets off the Plaza Circular near Calle Buenos Aires and Campo Volantín have numerous *pensiones* and hotels. Half an hour away by subway is the pretty coastal town of Getxo, next to the Puente Colgante, which has top hotels with views over the beaches, as well as cheaper hotels and *pensiones* in town. Reservations can be made at ⊜ infoturismo@getxo.net

HOTELS & GUEST HOUSES

You will find room prices advertised in hotel lobbies. The classification is by an official star system and noted on small blue plaques outside the hotel or guesthouse. Reservations may be made

PRICE CATEGORIES

Ratings used in this book are based on the average price for a double room per night, including breakfast.
£ up to €50   ££ €50–€100   £££ above €100

at ☎ 946 613 279 🌐 www.bilbaoreservas.com. The accommodation categories are as follows:

- *Hotels* Rated from 1 to 5 stars, based on their services.
- *Paradores* Usually historical buildings that have been restored as hotels; can be pricey in high season.
- *Hostales and Pensiones* Typically cheap and cheerful B&Bs, often run by families.
- *Agroturismos* Family-run farmhouses open to the public, usually located in beautiful rural areas.

HOTELS

Artetxe Hotel ££ A traditional Basque farmhouse on the hills overlooking Bilbao that's now a warm, family-run hotel with twelve rustic rooms. There's a restaurant serving classic Basque cuisine. ❸ Carretera Enékuri-Artxanda km 7 ☎ 944 74 77 80 🌐 www.hotelartetxe.com ✉ info@hotelartetxe.com 🚌 Bizkaibus 3216 to Artxanda

Barceló Hotel Avenida ££ Large (189-room), mid-range hotel that's geared towards business travellers and conferences, which means that weekend rates are usually moderate. It is near the Basílica de Begoña, just east of the old town. ❸ Av. Zumalakarregui 40 ☎ 944 124 300 📠 944 114 617 🌐 www.barcelo.com ✉ avenida@bchoteles.com Ⓜ Metro: Santutxu

Conde Duque ££ Comfortable 3-star Best Western hotel, located on the east bank just north of the Ayuntamiento and a short walk over the bridge from all the sights. The rooms are spacious and well serviced, and there's a restaurant. ❸ C/Campo Volantín 22 ☎ 944 456 000 🌐 www.bilbaohotelcondeduque.com ✉ reserves@hotelcondeduque.com Ⓜ Metro: Casco Viejo

Iturrienea Ostatua ££ One of the nicer choices in the old town, with a blue and yellow façade and plants on balconies. Housed in a lovely Basque townhouse, decorated in traditional style. ⓐ C/Santa María 14 ⓣ 944 161 500 ⓦ www.iturrieneaostatua.com ⓜ Metro: Casco Viejo

Ripa ££ A popular hotel with comfortable rooms of a generous size. The location is excellent – on the west bank of the river, overlooking the old town and within walking distance of the Guggenheim and the Gran Vía. Some rooms have balconies with river views. ⓐ C/de Ripa ⓣ 944 239 677 ⓦ www.hotel-ripa.com ⓔ hotelripa@teleline.es ⓜ Metro/Tram: Abando

Sirimiri ££ Small, peaceful hotel located near the Atxuri tram station.
ⓐ Pl. de la Encarnación 3 ⓣ 944 330 759 ⓦ www.hotelsirimiri.com
ⓔ h.sirimiri@hotelsirimiri.com ⓝ Tram: Atxuri

Vista Alegre ££ A 2-star hotel in the city centre close to the
bullring and within walking distance of most of the key
sightseeing areas. A hearty breakfast is served in the coffee shop.
ⓐ C/Pablo Picasso 13 ⓣ 944 431 450 ⓦ www.hotelvistaalegre.com
ⓔ info@hotelvistaalegre.com ⓝ Metro: Moyúa

◆ *Gran Hotel Ercilla's restaurant Bermeo*

Carlton £££ The most famous hotel in Bilbao, with plenty of history and some famous names in the visitors' book, including Ernest Hemingway. During the Civil War, it hosted first the Republican Basque government and then Franco's staff. Located in an elegant building near the Guggenheim. ⓐ Pl. Moyúa ☎ 944 162 200 ⓦ www.aranzazu-hoteles.com ⓔ carlton@aranzazu-hoteles.com Ⓜ Metro: Moyúa

Gran Hotel Ercilla £££ Hotel near Plaza Indautxu that's at the heart of the bullfighting community, especially during the Semana Grande in August. The service, facilities and rooms are top-notch. ⓐ C/Ercilla 37–39 ☎ 944 705 700 ⓦ www.hotelercilla.es ⓔ ercilla@hotelercilla.es Ⓜ Metro: Indautxu

Hotel Bilbao Jardines £££ Well-situated in the heart of Casco Viejo, the Bilbao has a classy, modern look. ⓐ Jardines 9 ☎ 944 794 210 ⓦ www.hotelbilbaojardines.com ⓔ info@hotelbilbaojardines.com Ⓜ Metro: Casco Viejo; Tram: Arriaga

Husa Jardines de Albia £££ Well-located hotel, just minutes from the Guggenheim, riverside walks, the old town and a metro stop. There's a spa and health club, and the rooms are of a good size and spotlessly clean. The buffet breakfast is excellent. ⓐ C/San Vincente 6 ☎ 944 354 140 ⓦ www.hotelhusaspajardinesdealbia.com ⓔ jardinesalbia@husa.es Ⓜ Metro/Tram: Abando

Mirohotel £££ Bilbao's first boutique hotel, designed by Antonio Miró and filled to the rafters with unique design pieces. Cool and comfortable, it's right opposite the Guggenheim and there's even a spa. ⓐ Alameda Mazarredo 77 ☎ 946 611 880 ⓦ www.mirohotelbilbao.com ⓔ info@mirohotelbilbao.com Ⓜ Metro: Moyúa

Silken Indautxu £££ A large hotel in the middle of the city, near Plaza Indautxu, that's housed in a handsome white building with a classy glass extension at the back. The interior is slick, and provides all expected 5-star facilities and luxuries.
ⓐ Pl. Bombero Etxaniz ❶ 944 211 198 ⓦ www.hoteles-silken.com
ⓔ reservas.indautxu@hoteles-silken.com ⓝ Metro: Indautxu

HOSTALES & PENSIONES
Pensión de la Fuente £ Small, family-run B&B in the heart of the old town. Some rooms are en suite, some have shared bathrooms.
ⓐ C/Sombrereria 2 ❶ 944 169 989 ⓝ Metro: Casco Viejo; Tram: Ribera

Zabalburu £ Family-run *hostal* with a friendly atmosphere.
ⓐ C/Pedro Martinez Artola 8 ❶ 944 43 71 00 ❶ 944 100 073
ⓝ Metro: Abando

Hostal La Estrella ££ Very good value for money and set in a delightful building with rooms of a comfortable standard. The location is quieter than other *hostales* of a similar category. Many of the rooms have balconies. ⓐ C/Maria Muñoz ❶ 944 164 066
❶ 944 167 066 ⓝ Metro: Abando; Tram: Arriaga

YOUTH HOSTELS
Albergue Bilbao Aterpetxea £ A 30-minute bus ride from the centre of town, this hostel has 48 rooms and eight floors. Facilities include a laundry, safe deposit, internet and a restaurant.
ⓐ Carretera Basurtu-Kastrexana 70 ❶ 944 270 054
ⓦ albergue.bilbao.net ⓔ aterpe@albergue.bilbao.net
ⓝ Bus: 58 from Casco Viejo, 80 from Termibus

THE BEST OF BILBAO

There is plenty in Bilbao to fill even a long city break but if you have only a few days to spare then here's our list of sights and experiences you should really try not to miss.

TOP 10 ATTRACTIONS

- **Bilbao Guggenheim Museum** The city's most celebrated attraction is worth a visit for the architecture alone (see pages 88–91).

- **Casco Viejo** Bilbao's atmospheric old quarter, full of charm by day and full of life by night (see page 66).

- **Poteo** Follow the locals and spend an evening sampling tapas, moving from one lively bar to the next (see page 34).

- **People-watching** It's traditional to chill out while enjoying the free entertainment provided by passing human life in all its variety, over a drink or a coffee, perhaps in one of the cafés of the Plaza Nueva (see page 71).

The Guggenheim Museum has been a key factor in Bilbao's regeneration

- **Puente Colgante** Bilbao's 'hanging bridge' is a miracle of 19th-century engineering (see pages 86–8).

- **Festivals** There's always a festival of some kind in Bilbao – whether a traditional religious occasion or a modern celebration of music and theatre (see pages 9–15).

- **Mercado de la Ribera** The largest covered market in Spain stands on the banks of the Río Nervión – search out bargains or superb local produce for a picnic (see page 71).

- **Shopping the Gran Vía** Shop till you drop in the department stores and boutiques of Bilbao's main thoroughfare (see pages 26 and 82).

- **Bilbao Tour** Get on the red double-decker and admire the city, getting off and on as many times as you want. ⊚ Lersundi 17, alongside Plaza del Ensanche ⓦ www.busturistikoa.com

- **Take the train up the mountain** The Artxanda funicular railway takes you out of the city's bustle to the mountain top (see page 80).

Suggested itineraries

HALF-DAY: BILBAO IN A HURRY

If you only have half a day to spend in Bilbao, your time will be best spent wandering around the Casco Viejo, taking in the sights. The old centre of the city is small enough to get around in a morning or afternoon and will give you a flavour of this Basque capital. The attractions include the cathedral, the Catedral de Santiago, the Church of Nicolas de Bari and the Teatro Arraiga. Save some time for kicking back in one of the delightful cafés, such as those in the Plaza Nueva.

1 DAY: TIME TO SEE A LITTLE MORE

A lot can be done and seen in one day in Bilbao but you will want to pace yourself. Devote the morning to the Casco Viejo, taking in the atmosphere, and the cathedral and churches. After lunch

● *Walking the picturesque riverside is well worth an hour or two of your time*

(remember that lunch here is usually late and leisurely), cross the Río Nervión at the Puente del Arenal, so that you don't miss the view across the river to the Ayuntamiento (town hall) as you stroll along the Muelle de Urbitarte towards the Guggenheim Museum, where the architecture and the art on display will easily occupy an afternoon. You could even forgo lunch in the old quarter and eat instead at the museum's excellent restaurant. You shouldn't miss 'el goog', but if shopping is more your thing, take a look at the outside and then head down to the Gran Vía for an afternoon's browsing in the shops and department stores.

2–3 DAYS: TIME TO SEE MUCH MORE

This allows some time to do both some justice to the sights of the city and take in a spot of shopping. Depending on your interests, you could happily devote a whole day to the Guggenheim Museum, stopping off in the café and restaurant. Another day can easily be spent on the other attractions of the city, such as the cathedral and the Museo de Bellas Artes (see pages 91–3), stopping off in one of the cafés en route. Explore the Casco Viejo, the covered market, the Mercado de la Ribera (see page 71) on the edge of the old town, or the Basque Museum. In the evening head back to the Casco Viejo for *pintxos* and drinks, followed by a meal in one of the restaurants in the old centre.

LONGER: ENJOYING BILBAO TO THE FULL

If you have sampled all of the above and have more time to spare, use it to explore the streets of the Ensanche, the northern part of modern Bilbao near the river. One or more days should be set aside for an expedition or two outside Bilbao: both San Sebastián and Vitoria justify a day or more.

Something for nothing

Much of what Bilbao has to offer costs nothing to enjoy. If you like museums, remember that many of them are free on Wednesdays or Thursdays (not the Guggenheim, unfortunately), and galleries are free. However, many other attractions are free of charge all the time – in particular, churches such as the Catedral de Santiago, the Church of San Nicolás, the shrine of the Vizcayans and the Basílica de Begoña (great for views of the old quarter).

Of course, there is no charge for walking the streets and soaking up the plentiful vistas and street life. You can easily while away the hours wandering the streets of the Casco Viejo or Siete Calles, the

🔻 *The Mercado de la Ribera, moored in the old town*

seven original streets of old Bilbao, the historical heart of the city. The old run-down quarter, near Calle San Francisco on the other side of the river, is being revitalised by a variety of new alternative shops selling books, furniture and clothes, and a variety of restaurants; check out Calle Dos de Mayo in particular.

Watching people come and go in squares such as Plaza Nueva, with its neoclassical arches, is a time-honoured Bilbao pastime. Sunday afternoon and evening is the time to see local families out and about. Another great place for people-watching is the daily covered market, the Mercado de la Ribera. Crossing the Puente Colgante (see pages 86–8), Bilbao's combined answer to London's Tower Bridge and the Eiffel Tower, is a great experience – the views from this 19th-century engineering masterpiece are fantastic.

When it rains

Unless you visit Bilbao in the height of summer (see page 8) you are likely to experience a rainy day, or half-day, but it doesn't have to be a washout as the city has many undercover attractions.

The Bilbao Guggenheim Museum, with its magnificent titanium architecture that seems to glow even on dull days, is your first stop when it rains. It could keep you occupied for a whole day of inclement weather, and you don't even have to go outside in search of refreshment, as the museum has a good café and restaurant.

However, Bilbao's museums don't end with the Guggenheim – visit the Museo de Bellas Artes at Parque de Doña Casilda Iturrizar, the Museo Vasco in the old town, the Museo de Arte Sacro or the rather eccentric Museo de Reproducciones Artísticas (Ⓦ www.museoreproduccionesbilbao.org). If you find yourself in the Casco Viejo when the clouds burst, hurry along to the Plaza Nueva or to a pórtico of Calle Ribera. The Mercado de la Ribera, the covered market by the river, is a fine spot to sample some interesting local produce under cover.

⬇ *Palacio Euskalduna reflects images of Bilbao past and present*

On arrival

TIME DIFFERENCE

Spain follows Central European Time (CET). During Daylight Saving Time (late Mar–late Sept), the clocks are put ahead one hour.

ARRIVING

By air

Bilbao's modern airport at Loiu, designed by Santiago Calatrava, is worth visiting for its architecture alone. Northern Spain's busiest airport, it is located 12 km (7 miles) north of the city. Facilities include four cafeterias, shops and a bureau de change. For car hire at the airport, see pages 63–4.

The yellow Bizkaibus A-3247 runs every 30 minutes from 05.25 until 21.55 from just outside the arrivals section, taking about 20 minutes to go into town, where it stops at Alameda Rekalde and Gran Vía before reaching the Termibús bus station; the fare is €1.20. Taxis are also available from outside arrivals – expect to pay around €14 to the city centre.

Bilbao Airport Ⓦ www.aena.es

By rail

Rail-based visitors coming from the UK via San Sebastián (see page 140) arrive at the Estación de Atxuri, which serves the Euskotren regional railway. This is located just south of the old town on the east bank of the river. To reach the city centre more quickly, alight at the suburban station of Bolueta, where there is an interchange with the metro to the city centre. Those arriving from other parts of Spain on RENFE (Spanish state railways) trains will arrive at the Estación de Abando on Plaza Circular, in the heart of the city.

By road

Long-distance buses arrive at the large Termibús bus station one block away from the San Mamés station on the west edge of the centre. The nearest metro station is San Mamés; there are also tram and local train connections. ⓐ C/Luis Briñas ⓣ 944 395 077

Most drivers will arrive from the direction of France on the A8 *autopista* (motorway). There are three well-signposted exits from the motorway into the heart of Bilbao.

By water

The ferry terminal is north of the city at Santurtzi and is connected by bus and train services to the city centre. ⓐ Av. Cristóbal Murrieta, Santurtzi ⓣ 944 839 494 ⓦ Bizkaibus A-3151, non-stop to Plaza Jado; RENFE: train from Santurtzi station to Estación Abando

FINDING YOUR FEET

It is easy to acclimatise to Bilbao. It's not a large city and the pace is manageable, plus the streets are laid out on a fairly regular rectangular grid (apart from in the old town), making it difficult to get lost.

Bilbao is generally safe for tourists, with lower levels of crime than the UK. ETA's ceasefire came to an end in June 2007; travellers should consult the Foreign Office travel advice (ⓦ www.fco.gov.uk) for the latest on the risk of terrorism. It should also be noted that traffic accidents figures are higher than the UK. Caution is needed when driving and also when crossing roads on foot; this especially applies to UK and other tourists used to traffic approaching from the right.

Levels of petty crime are lower than in the tourist areas down south. The usual sensible precautions are advised when walking

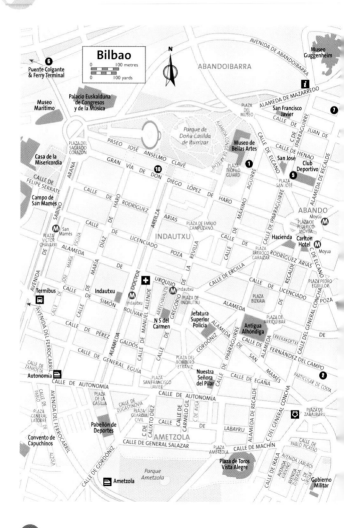

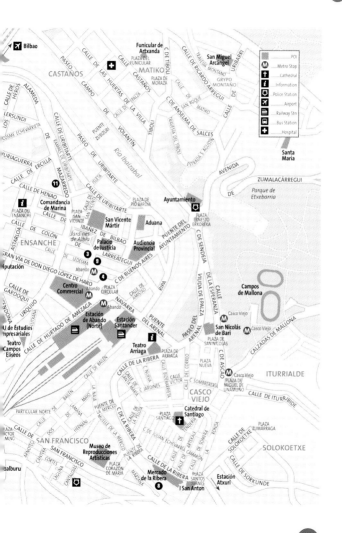

about the city, especially at night or alone. The red-light district
(or *barrio chino*, as it is known locally) near the Calle San Francisco,
south of the rail station, is not for the faint-hearted at night –
during the day, however, it is usually alright for wandering around,
with a variety of restaurants.

ORIENTATION

The centre of modern Bilbao is bounded by the river Nervión to the
north and east. It consists of a number of grand squares or plazas

IF YOU GET LOST, TRY...

Excuse me, do you speak English?
Perdone, ¿habla usted inglés?
Perdoene, ¿ahbla oosteth eengless?

**Excuse me, is this the right way to the old town/the city
centre/the tourist office/the station/the bus station?**
Perdone, ¿por aquí se va a el casco antiguo/al centro de la
ciudad/oficina de turísmo/la estación de trenes/estación
de autobuses?
*Perdoneh, ¿por akee seh bah ah el kasko antigwo/al thentroe
de la theeoodath/offeetheena deh toorismoe/la estatheeon
de trenes/estatheeon dey awtoebooses?*

Can you point to it on my map?
¿Puede señalármelo en el mapa?
¿Pwede senyarlarmeloe en el mapa?

linked by roads and avenues. The old centre, the Casco Viejo, is a distinctive quarter located on the east bank of the river. The Siete Calles, the seven original medieval streets of old Bilbao, are on the south side of the old quarter, encircled by Calle La Ronda. The Plaza Nueva remains the heart of the old city, where you will find cafés, bars and shops. In the middle of the old quarter stands the cathedral, the Catedral de Santiago, which is a distinctive feature on the Bilbao skyline and a useful landmark. The Mercado de la Ribera, the big covered market, is found on the east bank at the south of the old quarter. At the northern end of the old quarter is the district of El Arenal; here you'll find the San Nicolás de Bari Church and, opposite, the Teatro Arriaga and a tourist office (see page 151). Further up the east bank is the imposing town hall, and opposite Basque sculptor Oteiza's magnificent work 'The Ovoid Variation of the De-occupation of the Sphere'.

The banks of the Río Nervión are linked by several bridges, chief of which are the Puente del Arenal and Puente del Ayuntamiento. On the west bank is the modern city centre, called the Ensanche (Extension), developed to allow expansion across the river and now the commercial and business centre of Bilbao. The Puente del Arenal leads westwards to the Plaza Circular, whose distinctive feature is the tall grey building of the Banco Bilbao Vizcaya Argentaria (BBVA), dating from the 1960s. From the Plaza Circular, the Gran Vía is Bilbao's premier shopping street, running across the Ensanche all the way to the Plaza del Sagrado Corazón, where it meets up with the river again at the Puente Euskalduna, overlooked by the large Palacio Euskalduna conference and event centre. Just south of it is the home of Athletic de Bilbao, the San Mamés Stadium.

The westward loop of the river forms the northern boundary of the modern centre and at the northernmost point stands the

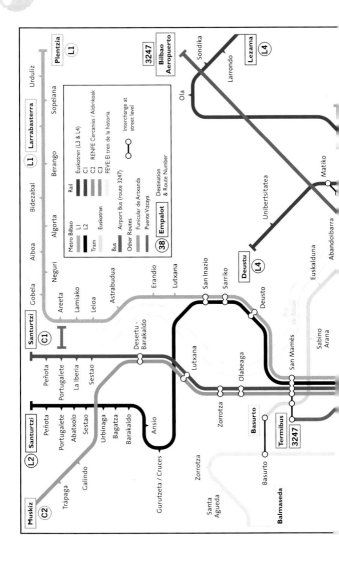

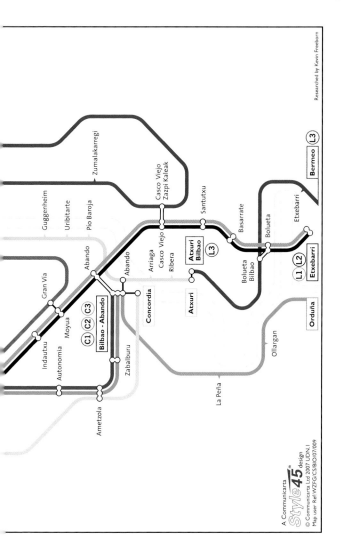

Guggenheim Museum; on the north bank is the centenary University of Deusto. Down the river, the 19th-century Puente Colgante links Portugalete and Getxo. The bridge was named a UNESCO World Heritage Site in 2006.

GETTING AROUND

Central Bilbao can be explored on foot without difficulty, since nearly all the attractions are within walking distance of each other. Nevertheless, if you need to cover the city quickly, there's a well-developed public transport system.

The modern, award-winning metro (subway) system has stations designed by Norman Foster; entrances to them are distinctive steel and glass tubular structures known to the locals as *fosteritos*. The two lines (more are under construction) run from the northern outskirts to Etxebarria in the south, crossing the centre of town with four useful central stops (west to east): San Mamés (by the football stadium but also useful for the bus station), Moyúa (halfway along the Gran Vía), Abando (at the main rail station and next to the Puente del Arenal) and Casco Viejo (on the eastern edge of the old town). Line 2 will eventually connect with the ferry terminal at Santurtzi (see page 55). Within the city centre journeys are a flat fare (€0.66). ⓦ www.metrobilbao.net

Complementing the metro is the even newer tram line. This usefully stops at some of Bilbao's landmarks, such as the Teatro Arriaga, the Guggenheim Museum, the Euskalduna Palace and the San Mamés stadium. You must validate your ticket before getting on. There are also red city buses run by Bilbobus, whose routes are displayed at *paradas* (bus stops). Flat-fare single tickets for trams and buses are €1, but you get a much better rate by using a *Creditrans* pass or by buying one of the multi-journey tickets that are available.

CAR HIRE

Driving Bilbao's traffic-packed streets is not recommended, but you may want to hire a car to visit some of the out-of-town destinations, stopping and making the most of the beautiful scenery and village life. Very often the best-value rates are obtainable by booking in advance through your airline or travel agent or on the web, but if you haven't done so and want to hire a car at the airport, try any of the following:

Avis ❶ 944 869 649 ❶ 944 531 209 🕒 07.00–23.30

Europcar ❶ 944 869 780 ❶ 944 710 000 🕒 07.00–23.30 Mon–Fri, 07.15–23.15 Sat & Sun

Hertz ❶ 944 530 931 ❶ 944 530 552 🕒 07.00–24.00 Mon–Fri, 07.30–23.00 Sat & Sun

🔽 *The distinctive metro entrances are easy to spot*

TRANSPORT BARGAINS

Sold in denominations of €5, €10 and €15, **Creditrans** is a multi-journey travel ticket that can be used on the metro, buses and trams (and probably trains in the future). Alternatively, buy a **BilbaoCard** from one of the tourist offices, which gives low fares on local transport and museums, and discounts at some shops and restaurants, leisure facilities and shows (one day €6, two €10 and three €12).

National Atesa ☎ 944 533 340 ☎ 944 530 359 🕐 07.00–23.30 Mon–Fri, 07.00–23.00 Sat & Sun

The local Yellow Pages lists many local car hire firms in the city centre.

◉ *The graceful Puente Zubizuri links the banks of the Río Nervión*

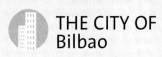

Old Bilbao

The Casco Viejo is the old centre of the city. The oldest monuments and sights are in this quarter, also known as Siete Calles after the seven founding streets. Its pedestrianised streets are full of Basque flavour with plenty of shops, bars and restaurants, as well as the cathedral, churches, the Basque Museum, and the nearby Teatro Arriaga and Paseo del Arenal.

SIGHTS & ATTRACTIONS

There are numerous sights and attractions in the Casco Viejo. The best way to take them in is by simply wandering around the maze of lanes, soaking up the atmosphere. In addition to the sights below, there are plenty of bars, cafés and restaurants, in particular on or near the Plaza Nueva.

Biblioteca Municipal de Bidebarrieta (Bidebarrieta City Library)

This wonderful building, erected between 1888 and 1890 by Severino de Achúcarro in an eclectic style, is one of the old town's finest structures. It used to be home to the Sociedad El Sitio, a society established in 1975 by liberals. The floods in 1981 caused serious damage but it was subsequently fully refurbished. A working library, it has a computer room on the ground floor with free internet access.
ⓐ C/Bidebarrieta 4 ⓑ 08.30–20.30 Mon–Fri, 10.00–14.00 Sat
ⓜ Metro: Casco Viejo; Tram: Arriaga

Catedral de Santiago (Cathedral of St James)

The first church on this site was built in the 13th century. It was expanded from the 14th through to the 16th centuries, which is

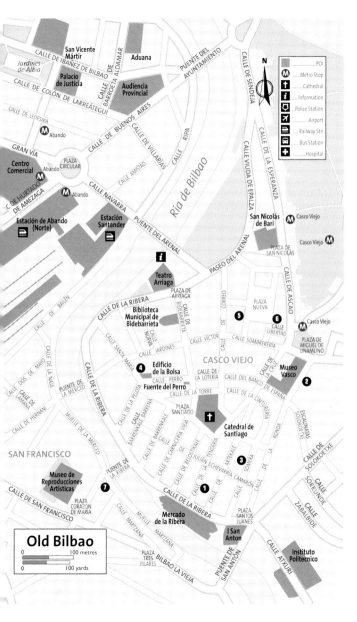

when the Gothic style was implemented, along with the portico, cloister, sacristy and the beautiful Puerta del Angel doorway, which contains a pilgrim's shell, the symbol of the pilgrims' route to Santiago de Compostela. It became a cathedral in the 1950s and remains a stopping point for pilgrims. ⓐ Pl. Santiago 1 ⓘ 944 153 627 ⓛ Daily ⓜ Metro: Casco Viejo; Tram: Ribera

Church of San Nicolás de Bari

Standing at the centre of the small El Arenal quarter, this is a church worth exploring. It dates from the middle of the 18th century and was constructed on the ruins of an earlier chapel. The octagonal baroque interior contains sculptures by the Basque artist Juan de Mena. Opposite the church stands the Bilbao Bank Building, the first office of the Banco de Bilbao when it was founded in 1857. Today it houses a cultural exhibition centre and historical archive. Nearby is the Paseo del Arenal, where a flower market is held on Sundays. ⓐ C/Esperanza 1 ⓛ Daily except during Mass ⓜ Metro: Casco Viejo

Edificio de la Bolsa (Old Exchange Building)

Built in 1725 to house the stock exchange, the baroque Edificio de la Bolsa is today a civic centre. In the building opposite you'll find a small figure of Virgin Begoña. If you stand by the figure you can see the Basílica de Begoña – the only place in the Siete Calles where this is possible, due to the old town's narrow streets. ⓐ C/Pelota 10 ⓜ Metro: Casco Viejo; Tram: Arriaga

Fuente del Perro (Dog Fountain)

This fountain, one of Bilbao's most popular sights, is a small and unusual neoclassical monument remodelled in 1800 from a previous fountain. Despite the name, it was constructed to provide drinking

⬤ *The late 19th-century Teatro Arriaga is one of Bilbao's key cultural centres*

water for humans, not dogs. People started to call it '*del Perro*' after the three vaguely canine-looking figures that form the spouts (they are meant to be lion's heads). The Calle del Perro is also a good place to find watering holes of a different kind – it's one of the old town's best areas for bars. ⓐ C/del Perro ⓝ Metro: Casco Viejo; Tram: Arriaga

⬥ *Take a well-earned break in neoclassical Plaza Nueva*

Mercado de la Ribera

A short distance from San Antón along the Calle de la Ribera, and located on the banks of the Río Nervión, is the largest covered market in the country. It sells local produce and is Bilbao's premier fish market, which is a big deal in a city that prides itself on seafood. The market building dates from 1929. After the flooding in 1983 it was refurbished and its interior modernised. From time to time the market holds cultural events, from theatre to exhibitions. 🕓 08.00–14.00, 16.30–19.00 Mon–Fri, 08.30–14.30 Sat Ⓝ Metro: Casco Viejo; Tram: Arriaga

Plaza Nueva

There are 64 arches around this enclosed square, built in 1821 in a neoclassical style. It's the perfect spot to take a break, with plenty of cafés and bars; it also has an outdoor flea market on Sunday mornings. Euskaltzaindia, the Basque Language Academy's head office, is on the plaza. Ⓝ Metro: Casco Viejo

Siete Calles

The very oldest part of Bilbao shows the shape of the medieval city, and is bounded by the 'round street', Calle Ronda, whose shape follows the line of the old city walls. At the southern end is the 15th-century church of San Anton, dedicated to the patron saint of farmers. Ⓝ Metro: Casco Viejo

CULTURE

Museo Arqueológico, Etnográfico e Histórico Vasco (Museum of Basque Archaeology, Anthropology and History)

The Museo Vasco (Euskal Museoa in Basque), housed in a building that was once part of a Jesuit church dating from the early 17th century, is an interesting exploration of Basque life, from pre-historical times up to the 20th century. It explores traditional ways of living, beliefs and occupations, both inland and in the fishing villages. In the delightful cloister there is a Mikeldi stone sculpture dating from the Iron Age. ❷ Pl. Miguel Unamuno 4 ❶ 944 155 423 ❤ www.euskal-museoa.org ❻ 11.00–17.00 Tues–Sat, 11.00–14.00 Sun. Admission charge (free Thur) ❿ Metro: Casco Viejo

Teatro Arriaga

The Teatro Arriaga is the most beautiful building in El Arenal, with a neo-baroque frontage. It is named after the 'Spanish Mozart', the Bilbao-born child prodigy Crisóstomo de Arriaga. Built by Joaquín Rucoba and Octavio de Toledo, it was opened in 1890 and is often said to resemble the Garnier Opéra in Paris. The façade has large balconies supported by Atlantean figures. In 1914 it was burnt down and has since gone through a number of changes. The magnificent interior, refurbished in 1986, contains antique furniture and carpets made in the Real Fábrica Nacional de Tapices (Royal National Tapestry Manufacturers). Today, the building functions as the City Theatre, with a full programme of drama, opera, ballet, music and other cultural events. ❷ Pl. Arriaga ❶ Information 944 792 036, Tickets 944 310 310 ❤ www.teatroarriaga.com ❿ Metro: Casco Viejo; Tram: Arriaga

RETAIL THERAPY

This is the oldest shopping area in the city. It has a large number of independent boutiques, as well as many chain stores, offering something for just about all tastes and budgets. The main shopping streets are Calles Ascao, Artekale, Bidebarrieta, Correo, Cruz and Somera.

Gili-gili Basque for 'tickling', selling unusual clothing and accessories for women. ⓐ Lotería 4 ⓣ 944 790 406 ⓛ 10.00–14.00, 16.00–20.00 Mon–Sat ⓜ Metro: Casco Viejo

La Iguana The owner chooses items he loves and mixes them up in this cosy shop. Find clothing, lamps and other beautiful items for the home. ⓐ Belostikale 4 ⓣ 944 155 146 ⓛ 10.00–13.30, 17.00–20.30 Mon–Sat ⓜ Metro: Casco Viejo; Tram: Ribera

Lu-la A colourful place where you'll find anything from women's clothes, shoes and accessories to items for the home. ⓐ Cinturería ⓣ 944 164 372 ⓦ www.lulabilbao.com ⓛ 10.00–14.00, 16.00–20.00 Mon–Sat ⓜ Metro: Casco Viejo

La Matilda etxeko pitxiak Home decoration and accessories. ⓐ Jardines 2 ⓣ 944 152 089 ⓛ 10.30–14.00, 17.00–20.30 ⓜ Metro: Casco Viejo; Tram: Arriaga

Skunk Funk Fresh-faced Basque fashion. ⓐ Pl. Nueva 2 ⓦ www.skunkfunk.com ⓜ Metro: Casco Viejo

Sombrerería Gorostiaga Founded in 1857 and still selling typical Basque berets (txapelas) made here, as well as a selection of other headwear for men and women. ⓐ Victor 9 ⓣ 944 161 276 ⓛ 10.00–13.30, 16.00–20.00 Mon–Fri, 10.00–13.30 Sat ⓜ Metro: Casco Viejo; Tram: Arriaga

Urbana T-shirts with attitude, clothing for men and women by up-and-coming young designers. ⓐ Portal de Zamudio 1 ⓣ 944 153 628 ⓛ 10.00–20.30 ⓜ Metro: Casco Viejo

TAKING A BREAK

There are numerous cafés and *tabernas* in the Casco Viejo, particularly along Calles Santa Maria and Barrencalle Barrena, and on Plaza Nueva. Many of the bars in the After Dark section below open all day and well into the night.

La Exquisita £ ❶ This traditional café and cake shop offers typical local sweet treats such as Carolina, a meringue cake named after the confectioner's daughter. ⓐ C/Tendería 4 ❶ 944 153 207

🔺 *The old town's best bars are often tucked away in alleys and hidden corners*

⏱ 8.30–13.30, 16.00–20.30 Mon–Fri, 8.30–14.00, 16.30–20.30 Sat, 9.00–14.00 Sun ⓜ Metro: Casco Viejo; Tram: Ribera

AFTER DARK

Bilbao's Casco Viejo is undoubtedly the choice place to head for *pintxos* and evening drinking, the best areas being on and around the Plaza Nueva.

RESTAURANTS & TAPAS BARS

Bar Baste £ ❷ A great tapas venue in the heart of the old town, famous for its stuffed mussels and Irish or Scottish coffee. The menu is very reasonably priced and represents exceptional value. ⓐ C/Maria Muñoz 6 ☎ 944 150 855 ⏱ 11.00–24.00 ⓜ Metro: Casco Viejo

Bar Motrikes £ ❸ This bar is located on one of the oldest streets in Bilbao but manages to combine a modern look with old-style stone walls and wood features. The grilled mushrooms are delicious. ⓐ C/Somera 41 ☎ 944 154 861 ⏱ 11.00–24.00 Sun–Thur, 11.00–02.00 Fri & Sat ⓜ Metro: Casco Viejo; Tram: Ribera

Taberna Txiriboga £ ❹ Tasty home cooking, including fantastic croquettes. ⓐ C/Santa María 13 ☎ 944 157 874 ⏱ 13.00–15.30, 19.30–23.00 Tues–Fri, 1.30–23.00 Sat & Sun ⓜ Metro: Casco Viejo; Tram: Arriaga

Zugan £ ❺ Tiny bar that has a huge range of delicious *pintxos*, and a great terrace with parasols on Plaza Nueva. ⓐ Pl. Nueva 2 ☎ 944 150 321 ⏱ 09.30–22.30 Mon–Fri, 10.00–23.00 Sat, 10.00–16.00 Sun ⓜ Metro: Casco Viejo

Victor Montes ££ ❶ This bar and restaurant with lovely *Modernista* décor and a terrace on Plaza Nueva serves Spanish cuisine; *merluza* (hake) and beef dishes are a speciality. Booking advisable.
ⓐ Pl. Nueva 8 **❶** 944 155 603 **Ⓦ** www.victormontesbilbao.com
Ⓛ 10.30–23.00 Mon–Sat **Ⓜ** Metro: Casco Viejo

◗ *You won't have any trouble finding this restaurant!*

El Perro Chico £££ ❼ Imaginative Basque cuisine over the river from the Siete Calles, next to Puente de la Ribera. It's said that Gehry came across his keynote 'Bilbao blue' in this restaurant.
ⓐ C/Aretxaga 2 ❶ 944 150 519 ❻ 13.00–17.00, 13.15–1.30 Tues–Sat
ⓜ Metro: Casco Viejo; Tram: Ribera

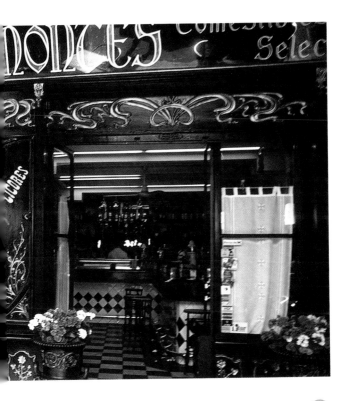

BARS & CLUBS

Badulake This bar is one of the best in town, on account of its dance floor, music (from the 70s onwards), and easygoing atmosphere. It's a mixed gay/straight venue. ❸ C/Hernani 10 Ⓦ www.badulake.net Ⓜ Metro/Tram: Abando

Café Bar Bilbao Good coffee and *pintxos*, and a nice terrace with friendly staff. ❸ Pl. Nueva 6 ❶ 944 151 671 ◐ 07.00–24.00 Ⓜ Metro: Casco Viejo

🔽 *You can't leave Bilbao without sampling the* pintxos

K2 A pub popular for its huge range of tasty sandwiches and photography exhibitions. There's dancing from midnight onwards. ✆ C/Somera 10 ☎ 944 163 450 ⏱ 10.00–02.00 Mon–Thur, 10.00–03.00 Fri, 12.00–03.00 Sat & Sun Ⓜ Metro: Casco Viejo; Tram: Ribera

Lamiak Studenty café-bar with good music. ✆ C/Barrencalle Barrena 7 ☎ 944 159 642 ⏱ 15.30–01.30 Mon–Fri, 16.00–2.00 Sat & Sun Ⓜ Metro: Casco Viejo; Tram: Ribera

Modern Bilbao

On the left bank, west and south of the Río Nervión, is the larger part of the city centre, stretching west and north from the Plaza Circular on the west side of the Puente del Arenal (for map see page 56). Most places of interest for tourists are located in the northern districts of this area, which are collectively known as the Ensanche or Extension, so named when, in the 19th century, the city's prosperity and industrialisation caused it to spread outside the old city. At its northernmost point, by the river, the old shipyard and docks area has been revitalised by the opening of the famous Bilbao Guggenheim Museum (see pages 88–91); further north, over the Puente del Deusto, is the Deusto district, site of the University of Deusto.

SIGHTS & ATTRACTIONS

Artxanda funicular railway

For a breath of fresh air, take this delightful funicular railway on the 800 m (1/2 mile) trip to the top of the Artxanda mountain (leaves every 15 minutes), from where you'll get panoramic views of the whole city and the river estuary. There are many restaurants and bars in the area, where you can taste *txakolis*, young white wines from the region.
ⓐ C/Castaños ⓑ 07.15–22.00 Mon–Fri, 08.15–22.00 Sat & Sun
Ⓝ Metro: Casco Viejo

Deusto

To get to the suburb of Deusto, either cross the Puente de Euskalduna (leading off Plaza del Sagrado Corazón) or the older Puente de Deusto, which can be reached from Plaza Moyúa via Calle Elcano. Stroll along the Ribera de Deusto for good views, especially of the Palacio

◆ *The Puente de Deusto, leading to Deusto University*

Euskalduna, the Guggenheim and Isozaki Atea. Located in this suburb is the grand-looking Universidad de Deusto, established in the 19th century by Jesuits. It is a prestigious place of learning, particularly in the field of business studies and law. The university has shown commitment to the Basque language, and created the first degree in Basque philology. It is located opposite the Guggenheim, and linked by a pedestrian bridge. The Deusto district caters to its student population with plenty of bars, cafés and restaurants. The district used to be a town, and it still holds to its old town identity.

Gran Vía Don Diego López de Haro
Modern Bilbao's main thoroughfare, named after the city's founding father, begins at the Plaza Circular and continues across the city centre as far as the Plaza del Sagrado Corazón. This is the shopping and business centre of Bilbao. Halfway along the Gran Vía you'll come

to Plaza Moyúa, a large roundabout with flower gardens at its centre and an attractive geometric layout. On it are two big buildings: the colourful Palacio de Chávarri, dating back to 1894 and seat of the Spanish local government, and the 5-star Hotel Carlton, which was the Basque government's headquarters during the Civil War. The Carlton, built in 1927, is on the city's cultural heritage list and is well worth a look inside. As you continue west along the Gran Vía, you'll be walking parallel to the Parque de Doña Casilda Iturrizar, the site of the Museo de Bellas Artes (see pages 91–3), and you'll eventually come to the Plaza del Sagrado Corazón.

The Nervión's bridges

The bridges over the Río Nervión, old and new, are key features of Bilbao's cityscape, offering interesting views. Most of them

◗ *Plaza Moyúa bisects Gran Vía*

are architecturally significant, and connect with riverside walks, enabling you to cross and re-cross the river.

Heading upstream from the Puente Colgante (Hanging Bridge; see pages 86–8), you come to the 1990s Puente Euskalduna, which curves high across the river and has a striking covered pedestrian walkway. The old Puente de Deusto is a bascule bridge, once essential for letting ships pass, and is reminiscent of London's Tower Bridge. Next is the pedestrian wood bridge that links the Guggenheim and Deusto University.

Puente de la Salve was a 1970s addition to Bilbao's riverscape. The original bridge was where Basque sailors could get a glimpse of the Begoña Basilica from the estuary, chanting a prayer to Virgin Mary, a pious custom recalled in a small monument. Today you can take a lift up here, which gives you one of the city's best views of the Guggenheim Museum.

The Puente Zubizuri, or White Bridge, is a graceful suspension bridge designed by Santiago Calatrava, architect of the new Bilbao Airport, and is named after the white concrete and white steel from which is built. It spans the Nervión between the Guggenheim and the Ayuntamiento, connecting Campo Volantín with Mazarredo over the Izosaki Atea. You can cross it to get the funicular railway up to Artxanda (see page 80).

Further upriver, the Puente de Ayuntamiento, or town hall bridge, used to be a drawbridge like the Deusto, but the mechanism hasn't been used for many years.

Palacio Euskalduna de Congresos y de la Musica (Euskalduna Palace)

This large, state-of-the-art conference and performance venue was built as part of the regeneration of Bilbao in the 90s. The shape of the building, designed by Federico Soriano and Dolores Palacios, represents the last ship built in the old Euskalduna shipyard on this site. Its auditorium can hold up to 2,200 spectators and has an extraordinary symphonic organ. The nearby curved Euskalduna Bridge was inaugurated in 1997. ⓐ C/Abandoibarra 4 ⓣ 944 035 000 ⓦ www.euskalduna.net ⓔ info@euskalduna.net ⓝ Metro: San Mamés; Tram: Euskalduna

Paseo Uribitarte

The esplanade starts opposite El Arenal and runs along the river all the way to Paseo de Abandoibarra and beyond, through an area that was once the industrial centre of the city (though few buildings from that period remain). As you walk along it, you'll see the new Isozaki Atea, the Zubizuri Bridge, Euskalduna and the Guggenheim; you'll also get views of the town hall to the east side of the river.

⊙ *Calatrava's Zubizuri Bridge makes an elegant approach to the city centre*

Isozaki Atea (*isozaki* means door in Basque) is a development designed by the Japanese architect Arata Isozaki, which comprises two skyscrapers and 1,000 sq m (10,764 sq ft) between the two buildings, where wide stairs connect the lower part of the riverside with the upper town. Halfway up take a look at Eduardo Chillida's sculpture *Looking for the Light*. Parque de Doña Casilda is nearby and along Paseo Uribitarte, you'll come across green areas and children's playgrounds. On the other side of the river there is an older, tree-lined esplanade called Paseo Campo Volantín, shaded by trees.

Puente Colgante
Bizkaia's most unusual bridge is up there with Bilbao's biggest attractions. The task faced by the city fathers in the 1880s was to build a bridge near the mouth of the estuary, which would not obstruct the passage of the large ocean-going vessels on which Bilbao's commerce, heavy industry and shipbuilding depended. Their solution, a transporter bridge, was opened in 1893, damaged during the Civil War (1936–39) and rebuilt in 1941. The bridge, whose iron structure is reminiscent of the Eiffel Tower, can also be crossed by the walkway on top, which affords splendid views of Portugalete, Neguri's wealthy neighbour in Getxo, the port and Abra bay. A new gondola was unveiled in 1998, the fourth in the bridge's history; its predecessors together had carried an estimated 650 million people and had made the equivalent of 31 round-the-world journeys. The new one will hold vehicles of up to ten tons in weight; per-person and per-car charges apply.

The gondola takes 90 seconds to cross and does so every eight minutes. If you have a head for heights, take the panoramic lift

▶ *Bilbao's transporter bridge has been named World Heritage*

and walk across (it's enclosed and safe). ⓐ Barria 3, Las Arenas
(Getxo) ❶ 944 638 854 Ⓦ www.puente-colgante.com
ⓔ transbordador@dominio.es ❷ 24 hours daily
Ⓜ Metro: from Bilbao to Portugalete or Las Arenas (Getxo)

San Mamés Stadium

Bilbao's 'cathedral of football' was erected in 1952 on the site of one
dating back to 1913, 15 years after the foundation of the Athletic de
Bilbao club (or *los leones*, the Lions, as they are known locally). It was
remodelled for the 1982 World Cup. ⓐ Felipe Serrate ❶ 944 240 877
Ⓦ www.athletic-club.es Ⓜ Metro/Tram: San Mamés

Teatro Campos Elíseos

This architecturally over-the-top theatre – an unmissable art nouveau
tour de force designed by Alfredo Acebal and Jean Baptiste Darroguy
– was opened in 1902 in an area called the Campos Elíseos (Elysian
Fields). Locals refer to it as *la bombonera* (the chocolate box).
ⓐ Bertendona 5 Ⓜ Metro/Tram: Abando

CULTURE

Bilbao Guggenheim Museum

The most famous cultural institution in the city has to be the Bilbao
Guggenheim Museum, which was built in 1997 and played a huge
role in the revitalisation of the cultural landscape of the city. The
ambitious project to bring part of the famous New York museum's
collection to Bilbao began in 1991, when representatives of the
Basque regional government approached the Solomon R. Guggenheim

▶ *The Guggenheim is guarded by Jeff Koons' irresistible* Puppy

GUERNICA

The painting that has stirred up the most controversy at the Bilbao Guggenheim is the one that isn't there: Pablo Picasso's *Guernica*, painted in response to the bombing of the town of the same name in 1937 by German bombers allied with Franco's Nationalists. The painting's symbolic importance to the Basques is huge: there was great jockeying to be the host of this famous work of art and much disappointment when the painting went to the Reina Sofía gallery in Madrid. Basques have been demanding the return of this evocative piece of art ever since.

Foundation with their plan to regenerate Bilbao and the Basque Country. The Trustees of the Foundation welcomed the proposal warmly, as it complemented their own plans for long-term international development to extend the collection. In its first year, the Bilbao Guggenheim had received over a million visitors.

The truly extraordinary building was designed by Canadian Frank Gehry and is a fine manifestation of his 'architecture is art' philosophy, mixing form and function to impressive effect. The giant sculpture with sensuous titanium curves is sometimes likened to a vast shimmering flower. Titanium was chosen as the building material to achieve a warm-looking surface that would glow even on an overcast or rainy day. Walk to the Puente de la Salve for a great vantage point from which to admire this remarkable piece of architecture.

Puppy, Jeff Koons' flower sculpture, can be found by the main entrance. This huge mountain of flowers has been adopted as an emblem of the city and you'll find *Puppy* souvenirs hard to avoid. Inside, there is a vast, airy and light atrium, leading to three floors of superb art from the last century. American sculptor Richard Serra's minimalist work aims to introduce the viewers to large-scale sculptures. Near the river is Louise Bourgeois' huge bronze sculpture *Maman*, which forms part of her 'Spider' series, representing maternity.

Free guided tours in English (limited to 20 people – reserve places in advance) are available at 11.00 & 12.30, 16.30 & 18.30 Tues–Sun. The popularity of this museum is phenomenal, so be prepared for queues, especially at the weekend There's a shop and café-bar on the first floor, and a good restaurant where you can try 'new Basque' cooking. ➋ C/Abandoibarra 2 ➊ 944 359 080; guided tour reservation 944 359 090 (09.00–14.00 Mon–Fri) ⓦ www.guggenheim-bilbao.es ⓛ 09.00–20.00 Tues–Sun; also open Mon in July & Aug. Closed 25 Dec & 1 Jan ⓝ Metro: Moyúa; Tram: Guggenheim; Bilbobus: 1, 10, 13, 18 to Plaza del Museo. Admission charge

Museo de Arte Sacra (Museum of Sacred Art)

This museum occupies the former Convento de la Encarnación, which was founded in 1515. Here you will find religious art and craft dating back to the 12th century, along with sculptures and paintings by Basque artists, and a huge collection of silverware from Spain and its former American possessions. ➋ Pl. de la Encarnación 9 ⓛ 10.30–13.30, 16.00–19.00 Tues–Sat, 10.30–13.20 Sun. Admission charge (Thur free) ⓝ Tram: Atxuri

Museo de Bellas Artes (Fine Arts Museum)

This gallery, at the end of Parque de Doña Casilda, tends to be overshadowed by its more famous neighbour the Guggenheim, but don't let this deter you. Art lovers will find it well worth a visit, with a collection of works by well-known masters, as well as pieces by more modern artists. You'll find works from the 12th to the 20th centuries by Goya, El Greco, Zurbaran, Rivera, Van Dyck, Gauguin, Bacon, and Basque artists, including Zuloaga and Oteiza, are well represented.

More than 300 works are on show from Romanesque pieces to 20th-century avant garde, arranged in chronological order, and the museum also hosts some interesting temporary exhibitions. There's a restaurant and a bar with good views. ❸ Pl. del Museo ❶ 944 396 060 ❿ www.museobilbao.com ❶ 10.00–20.00 Tues–Sat, 10.00–14.00 Sun ❻ Metro: Moyúa; Tram: Abandoibarra; Bilbobus: 1, 10,

13, 18 to Plaza del Museo. Admission charge (free on Wed); combined ticket with Guggenheim €12.00

Museo Marítimo (Maritime Museum)

The Ría de Bilbao Maritime Museum is located in the docks of the old Euskalduna shipyard, a stone's throw away from the Guggenheim and the Fine Arts Museum. It explores Bilbao's long association with the sea and shipbuilding. The permanent exhibition shows the evolution and heritage of the Ría as a seaport and shipyard. Outside there is a dock area with old fishing boats on display. ⬣ Muelle Ramón de

⬇ *Decorative heads on a fountain in central Bilbao*

la Sota 1 ☎ 902 131 000 🌐 www.museomaritimobilbao.org
🕐 10.00–20.00 Tues–Sun Ⓝ Metro: Sabino Arana; Tram: Euskalduna

Oteiza y Ayuntamiento (Oteiza and town hall)

The town hall's style, like that of the Bidebarrieta library, is eclectic.
It was built at the end of the 19th century by Joaquín Rucoba, who
took references from the classist style of the Third French Republic.
Opposite the town hall on a small square that marks the beginning
of the Paseo Campo Volantín, is Jorge Oteiza's sculpture, *The Ovoid
Variation of the De-occupation of the Sphere*, which represents the
artist's concern with emptiness. Ⓐ Pl. Ayuntamiento Ⓝ Metro: Abando

RETAIL THERAPY

The majority of Bilbao's department stores can be found on Gran
Vía. The big designer names, such as Gucci and Calvin Klein, are also
found along here. Don't forget the gift shop at the Guggenheim and
the Fine Arts Museum; both have a big selection of items themed
on their respective collections.

La Casa del Libro This bookshop has an extensive range of books and
maps, including English-language books. Ⓐ Colón de Larreátegui 41
☎ 902 026 408 🌐 www.casadellibro.com 🕐 09.30–21.30
Ⓝ Metro/Tram: Abando

El Corte Inglés The Bilbao branch of this renowned Spanish
department store chain should satisfy virtually all your shopping
needs, from luxury to everyday items. Ⓐ Gran Vía 7–9 ☎ 944 253 500
🌐 www.elcorteingles.es 🕐 10.00–21.00 Mon–Sat
Ⓝ Metro/Tram: Abando

For Men and women's clothes, mainly casualwear, made with high-quality fabrics. ⓐ Gran Vía 22 ❶ 944 356 302 Ⓦ www.for.es ⓛ 10.00–20.30 Mon–Sat Ⓝ Metro/Tram: Abando

Zubiarte Exclusive design and avant-garde architecture converge at this upmarket shopping mall with more than 70 shops. ⓐ Lehendakari Leizaola 2 ❶ 944 277 380 Ⓦ www.zubiarte.com Ⓝ Tram: Abandoibarra

TAKING A BREAK

Whichever part of the modern city you visit, you won't need much help in finding a café or bar where you can rest over a coffee or a drink.

Abaroa £ ❶ A restaurant with a big window to look out at the Museo de Bellas Artes. Traditional Basque cuisine. ⓐ Pl. del Museo 3 ❶ 944 249 107 Ⓝ Metro: Moyúa

Garibolo £ ❷ Cosy vegetarian restaurant with friendly staff. ⓐ C/Fernandez del Campo 7 ❶ 944 223 255 ⓛ 13.00–16.00, 21.00–23.00 Mon–Sat Ⓝ Metro: Moyúa

Café Bar Iruña ££ ❸ Dating from 1903, with a Moorish-style interior decor of coloured ceramic tiles, this remains a popular meeting point for a young white-collar crowd, and it gets busy from early morning until late into the night. Come for breakfast, lunch or evening drinks, when the music gets turned up. ⓐ Jardines de Albia 5 ❶ 944 237 021 ⓛ 07.00–02.00 Mon–Fri, 09.00–02.00 Sat, 12.00–01.00 Sun Ⓝ Metro/Tram: Abando

◗ The Guggenheim has first-class catering facilities

La Granja ££ ❹ One of the oldest cafés in the city, opened in 1926 and known for its elegant, old-fashioned feel. ⊕ Pl. Circular 3 ⊕ 944 249 059 ⊕ 08.00–24.00 Sun–Thur, 08.00–03.00 Fri & Sat ⊕ Metro/Tram: Abando

Kikara ££ ❺ Two-floor restaurant near the Guggenheim serving accomplished nouvelle cuisine. There is a non-smoking floor. ⊕ C/Iparraguirre 23 ⊕ 944 236 840 ⊕ 12.30–01.00 Mon–Sat ⊕ Metro: Moyúa

AFTER DARK

RESTAURANTS

Casa Vasca £ ❻ Value-for-money traditional Basque cuisine in the Deusto district. Try the spicy fish dish *bacalao al pil pil*, and for dessert *arroz con leche* (rice pudding). It's also a confectioner – try the delicious toasted croissants. ⊕ Av. Lehendakari Aguirre 13 ⊕ 944 483 980 ⊕ 07.00–01.00 ⊕ Metro: Deusto

Guggen £ ❼ Handily located for the Guggenheim Museum, yet more of a local hangout than a tourist trap, this restaurant offers a straightforward menu at reasonable prices. ⊕ C/Alameda Rekalde 5 ⊕ 944 248 491 ⊕ Lunch & dinner daily ⊕ Metro: Moyúa

Mina ££ ❽ Located opposite Mercado de la Ribera, with big windows looking out over the river bank, this restaurant decked out in wood and stone has a warm feel. The menu is seasonal. ⊕ Muelle Marzana ⊕ 944 795 938 ⊕ 13.00–16.00 Mon & Tues, 20.00–23.00 Mon–Sat. Closed Sun, Mon & Tues night ⊕ Tram: Ribera

Nicolás ££ Another good bet for traditional Basque dishes, especially fish, such as *bacalao* (salted cod) and *merluza* (hake). The bar also offers *pintxos*. ❷ C/Ledesma 10 ❶ 944 240 737 ❻ Daily except Sun evening ❻ Metro/Tram: Abando

Guria £££ A well-established restaurant offering upmarket versions of authentic Basque dishes in elegant surroundings. *Surtidos de bacalaos* (salted cod) is the chef's speciality. ❷ Gran Vía 66 ❶ 944 415 780 ❿ www.restauranteguria.com ❻ Daily except Sun evening ❻ Metro: Moyúa

Zortziko £££ A top-of-the-range restaurant in a historic setting. House dishes include roast fillet of grouper with truffle, scallops and vegetables with truffle oil. ❷ Alameda Mazarredo 17 ❶ 944 239 743 ❻ Lunch & dinner Tues–Sat, closed Mon & Sun ❻ Metro: Abando; Tram: Uribitarte

CLUBS & BARS

Central Bilbao has an abundance of clubs catering to all musical tastes. The area around Calle Mazarredo is a very popular night-time haunt, as are the pubs found in the Urquijo *galerías* (passageways). Ledesma and Licenciado Poza are good for bar-hopping, where the in-drink is *kalimotxo* (coke and red wine, invented by locals more than 30 years ago). Local favourites include La Granja and Iruña.

Azkena Specialises in live music, from reggae to rock. ❷ C/Ibañez de Bilbao 26 ❿ www.azkena.com ❻ Metro/Tram: Abando

Bar Poza 40 A lively place (with Wi-Fi) in Indautxu and a good place to join the locals watching Athletic de Bilbao on the big TV screen.

a C/Licenciado Poza 40 ☏ 944 416 639 🕐 08.00–24.00
Ⓜ Metro: Indautxu

El Caos Stairs take you down to El Caos, which – despite what the
name implies – has an easy-going atmosphere, and plays good music.
ⓐ Simon Bolivar 10 Ⓜ Metro: Indautxu

Cotton Club Monthly live concerts. ⓐ C/Gregorio de la Revilla 25
☏ 944 104 951 🕐 16.30–03.00 Mon–Fri, 18.30–06.00 Sat
Ⓜ Metro: Indautxu

Distrito 9 This gay club also attracts plenty of straight patrons with
its techno scene. ⓐ C/Alameda Rekalde 10 🕐 13.00–06.30 Thur–Sat
Ⓜ Metro: Indautxu

Palladium Not far from the Guggenheim, this is a good venue for jazz
on Friday nights. ⓐ C/Iparraguire 11 ☏ 944 246 165 🕐 08.00–24.00
Sun–Thur, 08.00–03.00 Fri & Sat Ⓜ Metro: Moyúa

Pas Pas Dance the night away at this club filled with sculptures and
silver columns, and the large raised dance floor. ⓐ C/Uribitarte 22
☏ 944 245 368 🕐 21.00–06.00 Fri & Sat Ⓜ Tram: Uribitarte

El Salero Modern, elegant place with white décor and warm lighting.
It's a restaurant, a bar and a place to relax. ⓐ C/ Manuel Allende 5
☏ 944 103 552 Ⓜ Metro: Indautxu

Santana 27 The biggest dance club in town, with four venues, each
with different music. It also hosts concerts. ⓐ C/Santa Ana M Bolueta
Ⓦ www.santana27.com Ⓜ Metro: Bolueta

Stromboli DJ sessions, art exhibitions and live performances make this easygoing central bar in the centre popular. Come for breakfast, a drink or a snack... ❷ C/General Concha 12 ❶ 944 051 872 🕐 09.00–24.00 Mon–Wed, 09.00–01.00 Thur, 09.00–02.00 Fri, 19.00–02.00 Sat, 18.00–24.00 Sun Ⓝ Metro: Moyúa

Wicklow Arms This small bar on Plaza Campuzano is where English-speaking expats in Bilbao get together on Wednesdays, Thursdays and Fridays. It serves the best Guinness in town. ❷ C/Rodriguez Arias 70 ❶ 944 425 148 🕐 12.00–02.00 Ⓝ Metro: Moyúa

▶ *Rusting chains on Bilbao's dockside*

OUT OF TOWN
trips

San Sebastián

San Sebastián, or Donostia, as the Basques call it, has to be one of
the most delightful towns in northern Spain, with an ideal location
on the beautiful Bahía de la Concha and golden beaches. It has
a French feel, and the aptly named Centro Romántico consists
of splendid old buildings. There are a number of beautiful parks
around the city.

Tourist office ❷ Oficina de Turismo, Teatro Victoria Eugenia,
C/Reina Regente ❶ 943 481 166 Ⓦ www.sansebastianturismo.com
🕔 09.00–13.30, 15.30–19.00 Mon–Sat, 10.00–14.00 Sun
Ⓝ Bus: 21, 26, 28

GETTING THERE

Up to three Euskotren trains an hour depart from Estación Atxuri in
Bilbao for San Sebastián (Donostia). You may find it easier to catch
the metro from the centre of Bilbao to the suburban station Bolueta
and catch the train there. Or take the bus, which is quicker and more
frequent. Buses from Bilbao's Termibus terminal (Ⓜ Metro/Tram:
San Mamés) take only 1 hour 10 minutes and leave every hour.
By car it's an easy journey along the A8 *autopista* (motorway) –
approximately 100 km (60 miles).

SIGHTS & ATTRACTIONS

The Parte Vieja is the old part of the town, by the sea and
overlooked by Monte Urgull, with its narrow streets, the Parque
de Alderdi Eder and a huge Ayuntamiento (town hall) dating from
the 19th century.

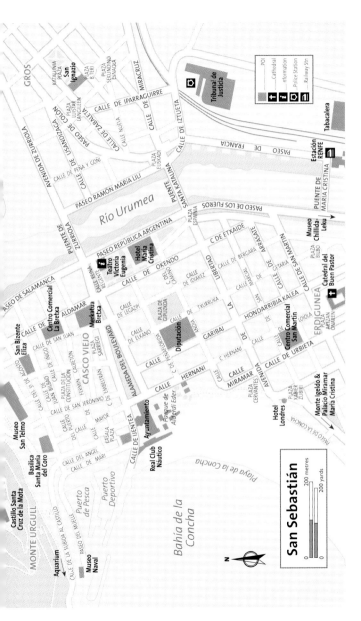

The Playa de la Concha is San Sebastián's biggest beach and it forms a golden swathe of sand, with delights such as the promenade of the Paseo de la Concha and the Palacio Miramar Maria Cristina, originally built as a summerhouse for the Spanish royal family.

A sculpture by Eduardo Chillida (see page 108), *Peine de los Vientos*, or *Comb of the Winds* – stands by the shore, just beyond the beach; it comprises a number of terraces built into rocks with cast-iron adornments, where the wind sweeps in from the sea.

Take the funicular ride from the end of the beach, where at the top you will be treated to magnificent views over the town, the Bay of Biscay and the mountains of Cantabria in the background. Alternatively you can head for the more stately pleasures of the Palacio Miramar Maria Cristina or Castillo de Santa Cruz de la Mota.

Alameda del Boulevard

The old fortifications of the city were dismantled in 1863, making way for this open boulevard, a pleasant place to stroll, relax and listen to music from the bandstand.

Aquarium

Children especially will love this attraction, which has a large array of marine creatures on display. An underwater glass corridor under the main tank allows you to get up close and personal with the stars of the show, the sharks Txuri and Urdin. The skeleton of a whale and model ships are also on view. ❷ Pl. Carlos Blasco de Imaz ① 943 440 099 ⓦ www.aquariumss.com ⓛ 10.00–19.00 Mon–Fri, 10.00–20.00 Sat & Sun. Admission charge

● *Playa de Concha is San Sebastián's playground*

CALLE 31 DE AGOSTO

31 August 1813 was a disastrous day in the history of San Sebastián. When the Duke of Wellington's Anglo-Portuguese army captured the city from the French in the Napoleonic Wars, the town was ransacked and torched (despite the fact that the Spanish were supposed to be on the same side as the British). Only the churches of San Vicente and Santa Maria and a few of the houses in the streets between were left standing. The fateful day is remembered every 31 August, when candles are lit in the balconies of this street.

Basílica of Santa María del Coro

Situated on the Vía Coro, this 18th-century church is a mixture of baroque and neoclassical styles. San Sebastián himself is depicted in a sculpture on the façade and there are a number of Rococo objects.

Catedral del Buen Pastor (Cathedral of the Good Shepherd)

The 75m (250ft) spire of this atmospheric neo-Gothic cathedral is visible throughout the old town. Finished in the late 19th century, the cathedral is situated in a square with relaxing gardens.

Maria Cristina Bridge

Inspired by the Pont Alexander III in Paris, the bridge is richly decorated with dragons, maritime scenes and coats of arms.

▶ *San Sebastian has centre stage on the façade of Santa Maria*

Monte Igeldo

Perched above the beach at Ondarreta to the east of the city centre, Monte Igeldo has over 6 sq km (2½ sq miles) of hilly parkland and is close to the rocky northern coastline. The quiet roads are ideal for walking and cycling. In contrast to the peaceful natural beauty, there's a funfair at the top of the hill, which can be reached from Ondarreta beach by funicular railway. Funicular ⏰ 10.00–22.00 summer; closed Wed & Sun in winter

Museo Chillida-Leku

Located 8km (5 miles) out of town, this museum is dedicated to the work of Eduardo Chillida (1924–2002), a leading sculptor of the Escuela Vasca (or Basque School), a movement that is rooted in traditional Basque culture. Chillida restored this 16th-century farmhouse and financed the museum himself as a place to display his huge sculptures made from granite and iron, which are set in 12 hectares (30 acres) of lawns and woodlands. ⓐ Jáuregui, 66 ☎ 943 336 006 ⓦ www.eduardo-chillida.com ⏰ 10.30–15.00 Wed–Mon

Museo Naval (Ship Museum)

This museum displays the long and interesting seafaring history of the Basques. It also highlights the important role that shipbuilding played in the development of the city. The museum is housed in the late 18th-century Consular Warehouse situated behind the port, in a building that was previously used as a guildhall for the ship owners and merchants of the town. ⓐ Paseo del Muelle 24 ☎ 943 430 051 ⏰ 10.00–13.30, 16.00–19.30 Tues–Sat, 11.00–14.00 Sun. Admission charge (free on Thur)

Museo San Telmo

This museum is located in an ancient Dominican monastery, dating back to the 16th century. A series of renovations have restored much of the church and cloisters, and the building has come to be regarded as a Basque national monument. There is a permanent exhibition on traditional Basque lifestyle, and also regular temporary exhibitions. The golden murals by Josep Maria Sert, a Catalan artist, depict the history of the Basques.

ⓐ Pl. Zuloaga ⓣ 943 481 580 ⓦ www.museosantelmo.com
ⓛ 10.30–13.30, 16.00–19.30 Tues–Sat, 10.30–14.00 Sun

Plaza de la Constitución

Known to the locals as 'Consti', this square is the focal point of the old town. It was once used as a bullring and the balconies overlooking the square were rented out to spectators. It is a hub of activity with busy terraced bars and a key party spot, especially during the festivals of Santo Tomás in December and San Sebastián in January.

Tabacalera

The new International Contemporary Culture Centre in San Sebastián is housed in a former tobacco factory, and the building's industrial aesthetics have been well-preserved. It explores cinema, television, contemporary art, design, science and gastronomy. Science and techonology are key fields, and the aim is to create a space in which culture, science and technology can interact. The building took 25 years to finish and the factory was in use for over 90 years, employing around a thousand workers at its peak. The tobacco company was privatised and in 2003 the factory was closed down.

ⓐ C/Duque de Mandas 52 ⓣ 943 011 311 ⓦ www.tabacalera.eu

TAKING A BREAK

You can get tasty tapas and seafood in most of the cafés and bars around the Parte Vieja. But finding a more substantial meal won't be a problem: San Sebastián has several high-quality restaurants, some of them rated among the best in Spain.

Ubarrechena £ This is one of the cheapest places to dine in the old town and is accordingly popular with tourists and the locals.
ⓐ C/Mayor ⓛ Daily

Beti Jai ££ This restaurant is one the best seafood restaurants in town, with seafood salads a speciality; meat and other dishes also served. ⓐ C/Fermín Calbetón 22 ⓣ 943 427 737 ⓛ Lunch & dinner Wed–Sun

Casa Urola ££ This is a splendid restaurant with a busy bar and a good-value *menu del día*. Popular. ⓐ C/Fermín Calbetón 20 ⓣ 943 423 424 ⓛ Lunch & dinner Thur–Tues

SPORT & RELAXATION

CYCLING

As an alternative to exploring the city on foot, it's well worth considering renting a bike. Keep a watchful eye open for pedestrians, however, as walkers also use the cycle lanes. You can rent cycles from the following companies:

Amara Bike ⓐ Pl. de los Estudios 2 ⓣ 943 457 367
Bici Rent Donosti ⓐ Av. de la Zurriola 22 ⓣ 943 279 260
Comet ⓐ Av. de la Libertad 6 ⓣ 943 426 637

⬛ *A sign of good seafood*

An alternative is to join a guided cycle tour:

Donosti Tour Tours on Saturdays and Sundays at 11.00, and at 11.00 and 23.30 during Easter. A guided tour of the city lasts about 90 minutes and costs €5. ☎ 943 481 166

Green Services Cycle rental and guided tours of San Sebastián and surroundings, including cultural tours and mountain bike tours. ⓐ C/Ramón María Lili 1a ☎ 943 260 598

BOAT TRIPS

Ciudad de San Sebastián tourist yacht Departing from the docks near the Aquarium, this 108-seater boat offers half-hour excursions around La Concha Bay and group reservations to other ports. Ticket price €7 (adults)/€4 (children). ☎ 943 281 488

Isla de Santa Clara ferry Santa Clara is a small island in La Concha Bay, and a popular picnic venue. The ferry service depends on weather conditions and the number of passengers and runs in the summer only. Ticket prices: €3.60 return (children under 8 free). ⓐ Departs from El Muelle dock behind the town hall ⏰ 10.00–20.30 June–Sept (depending on weather conditions)

ACCOMMODATION

San Sebastián is not a cheap place to stay. It's very popular with tourists year round; French tourists hop over for the weekend, or even just for a night out. The least expensive option is a *hostal*.

▶ *San Sebastián's fishing harbour is close to the old fortifications*

Hotel Monte Ulia £ Located in a quiet part of San Sebastian, just four minutes' walk from Gros beach. Neat rooms, many with balconies, a restaurant and free parking. Alcalde Jose Elosegi 21 943 326 767 www.hotelmonteulia.com contacto@hotelmonteulia.com Bus: 13

Hostal Parma £ Located by the Parte Vieja and Paseo Nuevo; some rooms have sea views. Paseo de Salamanca 10 943 428 893 www.hotelparma.com

Pensión Alemana £ This pleasant B&B is situated near the cathedral. The rooms are ensuite. C/San Martin 53 943 465 544 www.pensionalemana.com

Pensión Bikain £ This *pensión* with tidy rooms is located close to the beach and the Parte Vieja, and comes with parking. C/Triunfo 8 943 454 333 943 468 074 www.pensionbikain.com reserves@pensionbikain.com

Pensión Urgull £ Lovely, cheap option with nicely decorated and well looked after rooms, and pleasant views. C/Esterlines 10 943 430 047

● *San Sebastian's enchanting harbour*

Vitoria

Vitoria (Gasteiz in the Basque language) is the capital of rural Alava and the seat of the autonomous Basque Parliament. Vitoria flourished in the Renaissance, which left its mark by way of the lovely churches and palaces. The town was also hit hard by wars, such as the Peninsular War, and it was here in 1813 that Wellington defeated Napoleon's forces in one of his most celebrated victories. However, by the late 19th century Vitoria was once again flourishing. Despite its troubled history, the city has been impressively preserved.

Tourist office ② Pl. General Loma Ⓦ www.vitoria-gasteiz.org
🕑 10.00–19.00 Mon–Sat, 11.00–14.00 Sun

GETTING THERE

RENFE trains from Bilbao's Estación Abando go to Miranda de Ebro, where you change to catch a main line train to Vitoria. The total journey time is a little over three hours. Vitoria's RENFE station is on the south side of the city. Buses from Bilbao's Termibús station leave for Vitoria every hour, and take an hour. The bus station in Vitoria is on Calle de Los Herrán.

SIGHTS & ATTRACTIONS

The Casco Viejo, or old town, consisting of a series of concentric streets, is Gothic in character. These days it's a little run-down in parts but it has some attractive mansions and churches. The porticoed Plaza de España is lovely and a popular place to gather for drinks or a stroll, particularly in the early evening. Plaza de la Virgen Blanca, fringed by ancient houses, is a medieval square in the oldest part of

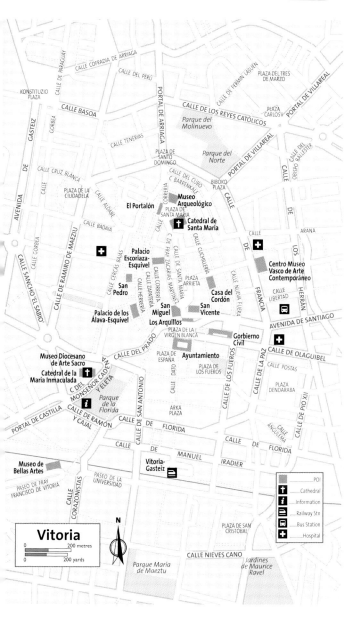

town. The San Miguel church dates from the 14th century and is worth a visit. Artium, the Basque Centre-Museum of Contemporary Art, has permanent and temporary exhibitions of contemporary art and a strong educational agenda.

Casa del Cordón

Currently undergoing restoration, this 14th-century Gothic tower is immediately adjacent to a 15th-century palace. The star-studded dome of the palace is one of the last remaining examples of Gothic decorative art to be found in the region. ⓐ C/Cuchillería 24

Catedral de la María Inmaculada

This curious building in the Parque de la Florida was constructed at the outset of the 20th century in a medieval Gothic-esque style, using historic building methods. It also houses the Diocesan Museum of Sacred Art (see page 122). ⓐ C/Cadena y Eleta

Catedral de Santa María

This fine old Gothic church on Calle Cuchillería is a source of great pride to the city – and indeed to the whole of Spain. It gave Vitoria a major feather in its cap by winning the Europa Nostra prize, the European Union's highest award for conservation. Visitors to the cathedral are encouraged to take a look at the ongoing restoration and to learn about the techniques used to preserve the architecture of the building. The cathedral has an exquisitely carved western doorway and a gallery built of stone around the naves, and the aisles have tombs dating from medieval times.

🄾 *The interior of the newly restored Catedral de Santa María*

THE BATTLE OF VITORIA

On 21 June 1813, in the countryside to the north and west of Vitoria, the Duke of Wellington's army confronted their French adversaries under Joseph Bonaparte, brother of the Emperor Napoleon. The fighting was intense and it was only after a long and desperate struggle that the French were defeated, leading to the capture of Vitoria by the allies. As was to happen also in San Sebastián, the victorious troops could not be restrained from looting the town afterwards. The human cost of the battle was the loss of 13,000 men, but the defeat effectively ended the French occupation of Spain and signalled the beginning of the end of French supremacy in Europe. The composer Beethoven wrote a symphony called *Wellington's Victory* to commemorate the battle. On a less elevated note, the British 14th Hussars captured a silver chamber pot from Joseph Bonaparte's baggage train. The pot is used to this day by the modern-day descendants of the regiment to make champagne toasts.

Church of San Miguel

This 14th-century Gothic church houses a number of interesting historic artefacts, including a statue of the patron saint of the city and, in the apse, the symbolic Machete Vitoriana, before which every new attorney general to the city swore an oath before taking office. The building also boasts a 17th-century altar by Gregorio Fernández and nine chapels. ❷ Pl. de la Virgen Blanca 🕒 Daily

Church of San Pedro
Constructed at the end of the 13th century, this, after the cathedral, is the oldest church in Vitoria, and has some interesting sculptures inside.

Los Arquillos
When Vitoria began to expand in the late 18th century, the city architects were faced with the dilemma of how to bridge the gap between the low-lying medieval town and the land that was to be developed. The solution that they came up with was Los Arquillos. These beautiful colonnades were constructed between 1787 and 1802. The first section runs alongside the Cuesta de San Francisco and the second along the Church of San Miguel. Along with the Plaza España, they represent the finest examples of neoclassical architecture in the Basque Country.

Plaza España
This fine example of 18th-century neoclassical architecture, with an impressive façade, was the result of the first major expansion of the city from its medieval core.

Plaza de la Virgen Blanca
A popular meeting point, the square of the White Virgin is overlooked by the Church of San Vicente, which bears more than a passing resemblance to the Catedral Santa María. Its 15th-century Gothic tower offers great panoramic views of Vitoria and the square hosts the opening of the fiesta of the Virgen Blanca in August, the city's biggest event, when the descent of mythical figure Celedón across the square marks the beginning of the celebrations (see page 124).

CULTURE

Artium: Centro Museo Vasco de Arte Contemporáneo (Basque Museum of Contemporary Art)

This museum, designed by a local architect, displays an intriguing array of over 1,600 paintings, drawings, photographs and sculptures from contemporary artists, as well as temporary exhibitions of more recent art. ❷ C/Francia 24 Ⓦ www.artium.org
🕒 11.00–20.00 Tues–Fri, 10.30–20.00 Sat

Museo Diocesano de Arte Sacro (Diocesan Museum of Sacred Art)

Located in the Catedral de la María Inmaculada (also called Nueva), this museum harbours a collection of religious treasures from the likes of Ribera, Luca Giordano and El Greco. ❷ C/Cadena y Eleta
🕒 10.00–14.00, 16.00–18.30 Tues–Sat, 10.00–14.00 Sun

Museo Arqueológico (Archaeological Museum)

The museum has a collection of finds from prehistoric to medieval times, with artefacts from the Bronze Age, Iron Age and the Roman times on display. ❷ C/Correría 116 🕒 11.00–20.00 Tues–Sun

Museo de Bellas Artas (Fine Arts Museum)

This gallery is contained in a wonderfully restored house built in the Renaissance Revival style of the early 20th century. It has a well-laid-out display of early art up to the time of Zuloaga, Amárica and Maeztu. It also has a decent collection of paintings by contemporary Spanish and Basque artists, the latter being especially well represented.

▶ *La Plaza de la Virgen Blanca is meeting point for Vitorians*

A sizeable collection of work is from the first Basque School of the mid-19th century, which shows 'costumbrista' pictures, paintings of everyday life that were very typical at the time. Contemporary Spanish art from 1950 to the present day forms the most extensive collection in the museum. ❷ Paseo Fray Francisco 8 🕐 10.00–14.00, 16.00–18.30 Tues–Fri, 10.00–14.00, 17.00–20.00 Sat, 11.00–14.00 Sun

Festivals

The Fiesta de la Virgen, the city's biggest fiesta, takes place between 4 and 9 August. For six days the city comes alive with impressive fireworks and outdoor parties. When the clock on the San Miguel church chimes 18.00 on 4 August, the mayor of Vitoria opens a firework display that culminates in the descent of a ceremonial figure called Celedón. A week of ceremonies, bullfights, theatre and general partying concludes six days later with the return of Celedón to the cathedral tower on 10 August to mark the end of the party.

Two other fiestas offer visitors an interesting take on Vitorian life. Dating back to 1482, the Fiesta of San Prudencio, held every 28 April, is heralded by processions of drummers in honour of San Prudencio, patron saint of Alava province. The Fiesta of the Blusa, or smock, takes place on 25 July. It's also known as Garlic Day – don't be surprised to see local people wandering around with strings of garlic around their necks.

RESTAURANTS

Casablanca £ A good menu of cheap and tasty dishes. ❷ C/Dato 38

Dos Hermanas ££ A well-known historical local restaurant offering very fine traditional Basque cuisine, including hake in white wine and more exotic meat dishes. ❷ Madre Verduna 10 ❶ 945 132 934 🕐 Lunch & dinner Mon–Sat

Ikea ££ Traditional Basque cuisine with a French influence. Specialities include foie gras terrine and Bresse pigeon. ❷ Portal de Castilla 27 ❶ 945 144 747

Mesa ££ This is a highly popular, reasonably priced restaurant. It provides no-nonsense tasty Basque cooking, with a good *menu del día*. ❷ C/Chile 1 ❶ 945 228 494

El Portalón £££ lautada itsaso, one of their specialities and the most popular dish, which mixes seafood, fish, lamb, mushrooms with various sauces. ❷ C/Correría 15 ❶ 945 142 755 🕐 Lunch & dinner Mon–Sat

ACCOMMODATION

Accommodation in Vitoria is easy to find except during the annual jazz festival in the third week of July or during the Fiesta de la Virgen at the start of August. The old quarter has the nicest options.

HOTELS

Almoneda ££ This is a recently refurbished, family-run hotel offering straightforward, elegant rooms with amenities. ⓐ C/Florida 7 ⓣ 945 154 084 ⓦ www.hotelalmoneda.com ⓔ information@hotelalmoneda.com

Dato ££ This hotel is situated not far from the station on the pedestrian thoroughfare and represents great value, with colourful bedrooms and furnishings, and bathrooms in all rooms. ⓐ C/Dato 28 ⓣ 945 147 230 ⓦ www.hoteldato.com

Hotel Silken £££ An opulent 4-star hotel in the heart of the city, offering everything expected of a high-end hotel. ⓐ Portal de Castilla 8 ⓣ 945 141 100 ⓕ 945 143 616 ⓦ www.hoteles-silken.com

HOSTALES

Antonio Casa de Huespedes £ Friendly *hostal* in an old building. Note that the bathrooms can be a bit of a walk away from bedrooms. ⓐ C/Cuchillería 66, Vitoria ⓣ 945 268 795

Hostal Florida £ A *hostal* close to the station, on the way to the bullring with comfortable, well-furnished rooms. More expensive rooms with a bath are available. ⓐ C/Manuel Iradier 33, Vitoria ⓣ 945 260 675

Pensión Araba £ Located right in the centre of the town, the Araba offers cheap and cheerful rooms. ⓐ C/Florida 25 ⓣ 945 232 588

⏵ *An historic arcade in Vitoria*

The Costa Vasca

The coastal route from Bilbao to San Sebastián affords some splendid scenery, with cliffs and great, wild sea views. Working fishing villages with some fine beaches (including Pedernales and Mundaka, which are well-known for surfing) are dotted along this stretch of coast.

A less romantic and more troubled spot is Lemoiz, which saw mass protests against the building of a nuclear reactor in the 1970s and 1980s – the project was abandoned in the early 1990s.

Castillo de Butrón

You pass this fairytale style castle in Gatika, on the way from Plentzia to Mungia. Built originally in the 11th century, it had a makeover in the 19th century, and is an impressive sight. 🕐 10.30–20.00

Sopelana

A haunt of surfers and hang gliders with breathtaking coastal scenery. It's also a popular spot to just hang out on the beach.

Plentzia

A traditional fishing port, Plentzia has successfully reconciled its past with the modern requirements of watersports enthusiasts. It's a great place just to relax, wander the streets and watch the harbour life. The Museo Plasentia de Butrón houses an interesting collection of maritime artefacts. For a good meal here, try:

Gaminiz £ Traditional Basque cooking in a pleasant atmosphere. ⓐ C/Areatza 38 ☎ 944 415 004

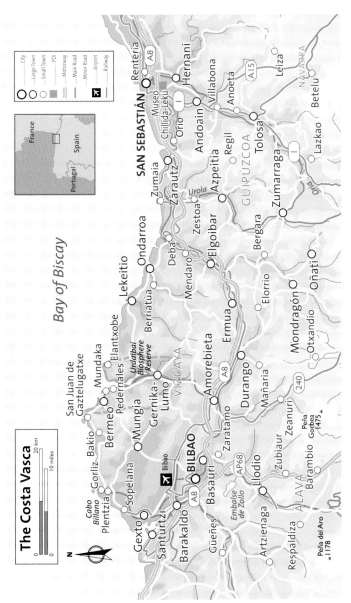

Gorliz

Another very popular beach, the main landmark in Gorliz is the lighthouse, a great vantage point for ocean views. You can also explore the small 18th-century fort.

Bakio

Bakio's two main claims to fame are *txakoli* and surf. *Txakoli* is a tart green wine made from a blend of local grape varietals (hondabarri zuri and belti, folle blanche and chardonnay) and was very popular in the 16th century. It is once again gaining popularity among the Basques, and you can visit the wineries in the valley inland from the bay. The 6km (4 mile) long beach at Bakio is becoming something of a mecca for surfers. Bakio has several restaurants offering hearty Basque food and good views.

Eneperi ££ ❷ Gibelorratzagako San Pelaio ❶ 946 194 065
Gotzon ££ ❸ San Pelaioko bide nagusia ❶ 946 194 043

If you plan to stay in Bakio:

Hotel Arimune ££ Centrally located on the beach, this an attractively quaint hotel has terraces overlooking the sea. ❸ Bentako plazea 1 ❶ 946 194 022

San Juan de Gaztelugatxe

This rocky promontory formed a starting point of the medieval pilgrimage route of St James to holy shrines of Santiago de Compostela. Joined to the mainland by a charming arched bridge, the isle has a 10th-century chapel, to which religious processions make their way on 24 June, 31 July and 29 August. The cliffs offer superb views of the sea.

⬤ The walkway to San Juan de Gazteluatxe

Bermeo

The town of Bermeo is a fishing port, with the largest fleet in the region, and is very much a working town. Fishing boats of many colours can be seen in the harbour. As you might expect, the fish in the restaurants is worth sampling. There is a fishing museum (see below) in a converted building beside the harbour, which gives you a flavour of local life and work.

Museo del Pescador This museum displays the history of the reliance on the sea by the Basque people. Tales from whale-hunting and trading are related here, along with a claim to have reached the Americas long before Columbus. ◐ 10.30–13.30, 16.00–19.30 Tues–Sat, 10.00–13.30 Sun

Mundaka

Surfing is big in Mundaka – it is the best and most famous of all of Spain's Atlantic coast surfing destinations. It does have another claim to fame though: Mundaka was the first town in the region to be mentioned in recorded history. It's a base from which to explore the wildness of the Biscay coast and the town also boasts maze-like alleyways and a splendid promenade along its waterfront. A passenger ferry runs twice a day (June to September) to the white sands of Playa de Laida.

Possible accommodation in Mundaka includes:
Mundaka ££ Family-run hotel with very friendly staff and comfortable rooms in a lovely old house. ⓐ Florentino Larrinaga 9 ⓣ 946 876 700 ⓦ www.hotelmundaka.com

◀ *Bermeo has the coast's largest fishing fleet*

Urdaibai Biosphere Reserve

UNESCO inaugurated this beautiful nature reserve in 1994. It covers 220 sq km (2,368 sq ft) of woods, marshland, beaches and cliffs, through which the river Oca runs. It is an important refuge and breeding ground for thousands of migrating birds.

Urdaibai Trust Information Centre ⓐ Palacio de Udetxea, Guernika–Lumo Road ⓣ 946 257 125 ⓦ www.urdaibai.org ⓛ 09.30–13.30 Mon–Fri

Gernika

Gernika is now a byword for Franco's atrocities. The town that symbolised Basque democracy and tradition was devastated by the fascists, with the help of Hitler's Condor Legion and the Italian air force. Around 250 people were killed and hundreds injured in a bombing raid that lasted three hours on 27 April 1937, market day in Gernika and so the busiest day of the week. It was the first action of this kind in world history and acted a prelude to World War II tactics.

The parliament building, or Casa de Las Juntas (ⓣ 946 251 138), is open daily and is free of charge. English guided tours are available by appointment and there are also virtual tours in English. Monday is market day and numerous farmers go with their best products to sell at the Plaza del Mercado.

Tourist office ⓐ C/Artekalea 8 ⓣ 946 255 892 ⓦ www.gernika-lumo.net ⓔ turismo@gernika-lumo.net ⓛ Daily

Museo de la Paz The Peace Museum provides a record of the 1937 bombing, using photographs, accounts and artwork. It's a pity that Picasso's famous painting hangs not here but in Madrid (see page 90).

◖ *Gernika's historic* Casa de Juntas

Two memorials can be found; one by Chillida – *Gure Aitaren Etxea*, or *Our Father's House* – and another by Henry Moore, entitled *Large Figure in a Shelter*. ☏ 946 270 213 ⓦ www.peacemuseumguernica.org ⓔ museoa@gernika-lumo.net ⏱ Tues–Sun. Admission charge

The Officina del Turismo has details of places to stay. Try these options:

Akelarre £ Nice centrally situated hotel on a pedestrianised street. ⓐ C/Barrenkale 5 ☏ 946 270 197 ⓦ www.hotelakelarre.com ⓔ akelarren@hotel-akelarre.com

Hotel Gernika ££ Traditional Basque-colonial-style hotel, built in 1963 but with a modern interior, near the centre of the older part of town. Accommodation is inexpensive but good quality. ⓐ Carlos Gangoiti 17 ☏ 946 250 350 ⓦ www.hotel-gernika.com ⓔ h_gernika@hotel-gernika.com

Gernika Youth Hostel £ In the outskirts of town with great views of the surrounding mountains. ⓐ Kortezubi bidea 9 ☏ 685 752 286 ⓦ www.alberguegernika.com ⓔ gernika@alberguegernika.com

Elantxobe

A delightful Basque fishing village that has barely changed with the passing of time. The village itself sits above the harbour, joined by a lovely cobbled street lined with fishermen's houses.

Itsasmin £ A nice hotel with restaurant. ⓐ C/Nagusia 32 ☏ 946 276 174 ⓦ www.itsasmin.com ⓔ info@itsasmin.com

❱ *Mending the nets at Lekeitio*

Lekeitio

This elegant fishing town has two very good beaches, near the harbour and across the river to the east. The town is very popular in summer, when local holidaymakers flood in from Bilbao. The 16th-century Gothic church of Santa Maria is well worth a visit, with its Flemish interior. Lekeitio has many bars and most have food on offer. For more refined eating try the following:

Kaia ££ Tasty seafood and views of the harbour. ❷ Txatxo Kaia 5 ❶ 946 840 313 Ⓦ www.lekeitiokaia.com

Meson Arropain ££ Great fresh seafood and fish. ❷ Arropain auzoa ❶ 946 840 313

Accommodation can be thin on the ground in Lekeitio but try:
Hotel Beita £ Basic accommodation at reasonable prices. ❷ Av. Pascual Abaroa 25 ❶ 946 840 111 Ⓦ www.hotelbeitia.com

Hostal Pinupe £ Conveniently located next to the beach, with basic rooms. ❷ Av. Pascual Abaroa 10 ❶ 946 842 984 ❷ pinupehotela@euskalnet.net

● *The magnificent 19th-century facade of Bilbao's Estación Santander*

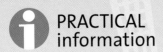

F-C DE SANTANDER A BILBAO

Directory

GETTING THERE

By air

Two airlines currently operate directly from the UK to Bilbao Airport. British Airways fly a twice-daily joint service from London Heathrow with Iberia, the Spanish national carrier; Easyjet flies daily from London Stansted. Flight time is about two hours.

British Airways 🕿 0845 773 3377 Ⓦ www.ba.co.uk.

Easyjet 🕿 0870 600 0000 Ⓦ www.easyjet.com

Iberia 🕿 0845 601 2854 Ⓦ www.iberia.com

Many people are aware that air travel emits CO_2, which contributes to climate change. You may be interested in the possibility of lessening the environmental impact of your flight through Climate Care, which offsets your CO_2 by funding environmental projects around the world. Visit Ⓦ www.climatecare.org

By rail

To reach Bilbao by rail from the UK you will need to make a few train changes along the way, so it will pay to carry as little luggage as possible. Frequent Eurostar services from London Waterloo International arrive at Paris Gare du Nord in about three hours. From there you need to take the metro to Paris Montparnasse station to catch one of the four–five daily non-stop trains to Hendaye, the last station before the Spanish border; these are fast TGV services taking approximately 5 hours 30 minutes.

From Hendaye catch one of the regional Euskotren narrow-gauge services to San Sebastián (Donostia); there are trains every 30 minutes and the journey time is 37 minutes. Change again at San Sebastián for Bilbao; the hourly service takes just under three hours and arrives at Estación Atxuri in Bilbao; however, it's usually more convenient to get off at Bolueta in the suburbs and continue from there by metro to the city centre. An alternative is to take one of the main RENFE trains from Irun to Miranda de Ebro and change there for a RENFE train to Bilbao, arriving at Estación Abando. Up-to-date details of these and other Spanish train services can be found in the monthly *Thomas Cook European Rail Timetable*.

◗ *Bilbao's distinctive tram*

Eurostar ❶ 08705 186186 Ⓦ www.eurostar.com

Euskotren Ⓦ www.euskotren.es

RENFE Ⓦ www.renfe.es

Thomas Cook European Rail Timetable ❶ (UK) 01733 416477;
(USA) 1 800 322 3834 Ⓦ www.thomascookpublishing.com

By road

Eurolines buses leave from London Victoria and arrrive at Termibús
in Bilbao. Most involve a change of bus and up to a three-hour wait
in Paris. The overall journey time is about 22 hours.

National Express Ⓦ www.nationalexpress.com

Bilbao is approximately 2,000km (1,375 miles) by road from Calais,
mostly on (toll-paying) motorways. The shortest route is via Paris,
Orléans, Poitiers and Bordeaux, crossing the border near San Sebastián
and continuing on the A8 motorway to Bilbao.

Cars must carry a warning triangle, spare bulbs and a first-aid
kit. Headlamps must be adjusted for right-hand driving. Your motor
insurance has to be valid for travel in Spain and you need a valid
national driving licence (an international licence is not necessary).

By water

As well as the direct ferry route to Bilbao with P&O, Brittany Ferries
offers the alternative of sailing with your car to Santander, further
along the Basque coast and driving on to Bilbao along the
A8 motorway, a distance of 103km (64 miles).

Brittany Ferries Sailings from Plymouth to Santander. The crossing
takes 24 hours and operates on Monday and Wednesday April–mid
September, Wednesday and Sunday mid Sept–Mar. ❶ 08705 360 360
Ⓦ www.brittanyferries.co.uk

P&O Ferries Sailings from Portsmouth to Bilbao on a large ferry with accommodation for passengers and cars, cabins and leisure facilities. Departs 20.00 from Portsmouth on Tuesday and Saturday and returns from Bilbao at 12.30 on Monday and Thursday. The Spanish terminal is at Santurzi, which is 13 km (8 miles) from Bilbao. ❶ 0870 2424 999/0990 980 555 Ⓦ www.poferries.com

ENTRY FORMALITIES

Citizens of the UK, Republic of Ireland, other EU countries, the USA, Canada, Australia and New Zealand are all permitted to enter Spain with a valid passport. A visa is required if the duration of the stay is more than 90 days. Visitors from South Africa need to ensure that they have a valid passport and visa, return or onward travel tickets and sufficient funds for their stay.

Visitors to Spain from within the EU are entitled to bring their personal effects and goods for personal consumption and not for resale, which can be up to 800 cigarettes and ten litres of spirits. Those entering the country from outside the EU may bring 200 cigarettes (50 cigars, 250g tobacco), two litres of wine or one litre of spirits. No meat or dairy products are allowed to be brought into the country from inside or outside the EU.

MONEY

Since 2002 the currency in Spain has been the euro. Easily distinguishable notes are available in denominations of 5, 10, 20, 50 and 100 euros, while coins worth 1, 2, 5, 10, 20 and 50 cents, as well as 1 and 2 euros are widely used.

There are plenty of banks (*bancos*) and savings banks (*caixes d'estalvis/cajas de ahorros*) in the city, except in the winding streets of the historic centre. Tourist hotspots such as Plaza Circular and the

◔ Bilbao's distinct street signs tell you where you are

shopping streets are well-served by banks and ATMs. The most convenient option is to obtain cash from one of the numerous ATMs attached to the bank buildings with your debit or credit card. Almost all ATMs in Bilbao accept international cards, but your bank is likely to charge a fee for such withdrawals. All of the banks will accept traveller's cheques (with your passport), but will charge a commission. There are also bureaux de change offices in the same tourist areas as the banks and while some of them may not charge commission, their exchange rate will usually be lower.

Credit cards are generally accepted in the city's hotels, shops and restaurants, but don't assume that smaller establishments and museums will take plastic payment. If in any doubt, ask before embarrassment occurs.

HEALTH, SAFETY & CRIME

Bilbao's drinking water is declared safe by the government, but many people prefer to drink bottled water for taste reasons. Bear this in mind when waiters try and persuade you into drinking bottled water in restaurants. The city's food should present no health risk to travellers.

Spain's public healthcare system is very good and thanks to a reciprocal agreement, citizens of the UK and other EU countries are entitled to free medical treatment following the presentation of a valid European Health Insurance Card (EHIC). The EHIC is not accepted by private medical practices in Spain and does not entitle holders to free dental treatment (except emergency extractions). Apply for the EHIC on-line at ⓦ www.dh.gov.uk/travellers and allow at least a week to receive the card. It is standard practice in Spanish hospitals to request ID from patients, so make sure that you have your passport with you.

Remember that the EHIC is no substitute for personal medical insurance and will not cover repatriation for medical treatment. Nationals of non-EU countries should ensure that they have adequate medical cover before travelling.

Tourists in Bilbao are not often the victims of crime and it is a safe place to visit, but keep an eye on your valuables in busy areas, because pickpockets will always be on the lookout for an easy target. There are two police forces, but you will not encounter them often on the street; the **Policía Local** deal with minor matters, such as traffic offences and wear a blue-and-white uniform, while the blue-uniformed **Policía Nacional** deal with weightier problems like drugs and terrorism. See Emergencies (page 152) for more details.

Basque Spain is generally safe, with lower levels of crime than the UK. The usual, sensible precautions are advised when travelling. ETA's ceasefire was renounced in June 2007, and terrorist threats from other directions are always a possibility here, as in all other parts of the world, so you should apply the same degree of caution (about unattended bags, for instance) as you would at home.

OPENING HOURS

Shops and offices tend to be open between 09.30 and 13.30 or 14.30, with a two–three-hour closure before reopening at 16.00, closing again at 20.00. Banking hours vary – most banks open Monday to Friday 09.00–14.00 and Saturdays 09.00–12.30. They are always closed on Sundays and public holidays.

TOILETS

Public toilets (*servicios* or *aseos*) are increasing in number in northern Spain but are still not plentiful. In an emergency you can nip into a café or bar, but it is polite to patronise the establishment afterwards, even if you only buy a coffee. The standard of public facilities is not uniformly high but those in major museums are generally fine.

CHILDREN

Children are widely welcomed and warmly regarded by the family-oriented Basques, as with elsewhere in Spain. It is quite common to see children eating out with the rest of the family in restaurants even late at night (though tapas bars and clubs are not suitable for children). The kids may not be happy to tour round many museums

○ *Children of all ages love a puppet show*

or churches, but they'll love the *Puppy* sculpture at the Guggenheim and a ride in the gondola of the Puente Colgante or the Artxanda funicular is sure to appeal to the older ones. The beaches of San Sebastián and other parts of the Basque coast are ideal for families, of course. All but very young children will also love the quirkiness, the fireworks and the spontaneous fun of the region's many festivals, though take care to keep an eye on them in street crowds.

Other activities, specifically laid on for children, include:

- **Kafe Antzokia** This Basque-language cultural and music centre devotes Sunday afternoons to performances for young children, including clowns, puppet shows and children's theatre. During the day it is a restaurant with a menu, and at night a concert hall. ⓐ C/San Vicente 2 ❶ 944 244 625 ⓦ www.kafeantzokia.com

- **Guggenheim Museum** Activities and workshops for children at weekends, which must be booked in advance. Free guided tours for families and children aged 6–12, 12.00–13.00 Sun. ⓐ Av. Abandoibarra 2 ❶ 944 359 090

- **Gran Circo Mundial** During the Semana Grande festival in August the 'great world circus' comes to Bilbao and sets up in the Parque de Etxebarría.

- **Karpin Abentura** This environmentally aware theme park in Karrantza (50 km west of Bilbao) has attractions including Iberian and European fauna, animated dinosaur shows, recreational areas, exhibitions and restaurants. ⓐ Biañez auzoa ❶ 944 479 206 ⓔ iniciativas@inicitivasambientales.es ⓦ www.karpinabentura.com

COMMUNICATIONS

Phone

Coin- and card-operated telephone booths can be found all over the city. Phone cards (*tarjeta telefónica*) can be purchased at tobacconists and newsagents. Any phone booth marked *telefono internacional* can be used to make calls abroad; it is cheaper to call before 08.00 or after 22.00. To phone home, dial the access code 00, then your national code (44 for the UK, 353 Republic of Ireland, 1 USA or Canada, 61 Australia, 64 New Zealand, 27 South Africa) plus the area code (minus the first 0 in UK codes), and then the rest of the number.

For international operator assistance, dial 11825 for information on international calls.

The Bilbao and other Spanish numbers quoted in this book include the local area code, a three-digit number followed by a six-digit number. Dial the full number for calls from within Spain. To call Spain from abroad dial the international access code (00 in the UK, for instance), followed by 34, the code for Spain, and then the number as shown in this book. For Spanish directory enquiries dial 11888.

Post

Post offices (*correos*) are open 08.30–20.30 Mon–Fri and 09.00–13.00 Sat, but those times may vary, especially in the summer. The main post offices can be found in front of the Guggenheim at C/Abandoibarra 2 and at Paseo de Arenal (🕐 09.00–14.00, 16.00–19.30 Mon–Fri, 09.00–14.00 Sat, 10.00–14.00 Sun).

Stamps (*sellos*) can also be bought in tobacconists. Mail boxes are a bright yellow colour. Mail from Spain is usually reliable and postcards take about five days to reach the UK.

Internet cafés
Cybercafés in the city include:
Antxi ⊜ C/Luis Briñas 13
Laser Centre ⊜ Sendeja 5; Wifi area: Kaldarapeko C/Perro 1

ELECTRICITY
Current is 225 AC, 220V and plugs are the continental two-pin type.
Visitors from the UK will need a three-pin adapter; visitors from
North America will need a transformer to adapt the voltage.

TRAVELLERS WITH DISABILITIES
Only limited facilities are available for travellers with disabilities,
though some accessible accommodation is provided. The Bilbao
tourist office has information sheets for people with disabilities.
RENFE, the state rail company, provides wheelchairs at stations.
 Sources of UK advice for travellers with disabilities include:
Disabled Persons Transport Advisory Committee
Ⓦ www.dptac.gov.uk/door-to-door
Trip Scope ⓣ 08457 585641 Ⓦ www.tripscope.org.uk

TOURIST INFORMATION
Bilbao Turismo Offices
The city tourist authority maintains three helpful offices in the city:
Ensanche ⊜ Pl. Ensanche 11 ⓣ 944 795 760 ⓕ 944 795 761
ⓔ informacion@bilbaoturismo.bilbao.net ⓛ 09.00–14.00,
16.00–19.30 Mon–Fri
Abando ⊜ Av. Abandoibarra 2 ⓛ 11.00–14.30, 15.30–18.00 Tues–Fri,
11.00–15.00, 16.00–19.00 Sat, 11.00–14.00 Sun & public holidays.

Old town ⒶPlaza Arriaga (behind the Teatro Arriaga) 🕐 09.30–14.00, 16.00–19.30 Mon–Sat; 09.30–14.00 Sun & public holidays

Bilbao Turismo publishes an informative guide, called simply *Bilbao Guide*, every two months (available from the above addresses), which is especially good for information on the latest festivals, pop concerts and events in general.

Websites
Bilbao The city's informative tourism website is at Ⓦ www.bilbao.net
Basque Country Visit the tourism website for the Basque provinces of Bizkaia, Gipuzkoa and Araba Ⓦ www.basquecountry-tourism.com

BACKGROUND READING
The 'Guggenheim effect', the story of how the imagination and vision behind the building of this iconic museum helped rescue the city's declining industrial economy, is described in *The Guggenheim Museum Bilbao: Transforming a City by Georgene Poulakidas* (High Interest Books). One of the best introductions to Basque culture, showing how extensively this small nation has contributed to European and world culture, is *The Basque History of the World: The Story of a Nation* by Mark Kurlansky (Walker & Co).

Emergencies

EMERGENCY NUMBERS
Ambulance and all-purpose number for emergencies ❶ 112
Police ❶ 091
Fire service ❶ 080
Emergencias Osakidetza (Basque health service emergency number)
❶ 944 100 000

MEDICAL SERVICES
In an emergency you should ask to be taken to the nearest *hospital urgencies* or *hospital de la seguridad social*. Under Spanish law, any health organisation, public or private, is required to treat patients in an emergency situation, regardless of their insurance status. However, emergency may be defined as a question of life and death – the responsibility of deciding what constitutes an emergency rests with the nurse or doctor on call. Holders of EHIC cards (see page 145) are entitled to basic medical treatment in any case, but travel insurance with a high level of cover is still advisable, and essential for non-EU visitors.

The emergency medical services are extremely good. You should try and give the age of the patient and type of emergency if calling 112, so that the ambulance can have a doctor on board if necessary. Some useful words are *ataque cardiaco* (heart attack), *ambulancia* (ambulance) and *médico* (doctor). By law, taxis are obliged to transport medical emergencies to hospital when requested to do so.

If you are physically able, you can go to a hospital emergency or casualty department (*urgencia*) or a 24-hour public health clinic. The telephone numbers of first-aid stations are listed at the front of telephone directories and many are equipped with ambulances.

Most pharmacies post a list of local clinics and hospitals where emergency medical treatment is available.

The following are the most central hospitals in the Bilbao area:

Hospital de Basurto ⓐ Av. Montevideo 18 ⓣ 944 006 000.

Hospital de Cruces (Barakaldo) ⓐ Pl. Cruces ⓣ 946 006 000

Hospital de Galdakao (Galdakao) ⓐ Labeaga ⓣ 944 007 000

Hospital Santa Marina ⓐ Carretera de Santa Marina 41 ⓣ 944 006 900

If you need a doctor or medicine in a non-urgent situation and are unable to contact a doctor, ring the telephone information number ⓣ 1003 or a police station, either of whom will give you the telephone number of a doctor on call or the address of the pharmacy that is open. Usually the hotel you are staying in should be able to advise you. For a list of English-speaking doctors, the best advice can be obtained from local tourist offices or your embassy or consulate. For minor complaints you can visit a pharmacy (*farmacia*). Spanish pharmacies have qualified staff who can offer advice and help on complaints for which you would consult a doctor at home. Pharmacy opening hours are 09.00–13.00, 16.00–19.00, and there is always a pharmacy that operates outside those hours.

EMBASSIES & CONSULATES

Australian Embassy ⓐ Pl. del Descubridor Diego de Ordas 3, Madrid ⓣ 913 536 600 ⓕ 913 536 692

Canadian Consulate ⓐ Plaça de Catalunya 9, Barcelona ⓣ 934 127 236

New Zealand Embassy ⓐ Pl. de la Lealtad 2, Madrid ⓣ 915 230 226 ⓕ 915 230 171

Republic of Ireland Consulate ⊜ C/Elcano 5, 1st floor, Bilbao
☎ 944 230 414
South African Consulate ⊜ C/Las Mercedes 31, 4th floor, apt. 2,
Las Arenas, Getxo, Bilbao ☎ 944 641 124.
UK British Consulate ⊜ Alameda Urquijo 2, 8th floor, Bilbao
☎ 944 157 600
US Embassy ⊜ C/Serrano 75, Madrid ☎ 915 872 240 ☎ 915 872 243

EMERGENCY PHRASES

Help! ¡Socorro! *¡Sawkoro!*
Fire! ¡Fuego! *¡Fwegoh!*
Stop! ¡Stop! *¡Stop!*

Call an ambulance/a doctor/the police/the fire service!
¡Llame a una ambulancia/un médico/la policía/a los bomberos!
¡Lliame a oona anboolanthea/oon meydico/la poletheea/
a lohs bombehrohs!

◗ *The Guggenheim Museum dominates the city of Bilbao*

WHAT'S IN YOUR GUIDEBOOK?

Independent authors Impartial up-to-date information from our travel experts who meticulously source local knowledge.

Experience Thomas Cook's 165 years in the travel industry and guidebook publishing enriches every word with expertise you can trust.

Travel know-how Contributions by thousands of staff around the globe, each one living and breathing travel.

Editors Travel-publishing professionals, pulling everything together to craft a perfect blend of words, pictures, maps and design.

You, the traveller We deliver a practical, no-nonsense approach to information, geared to how you really use it.

SPOT A CITY IN SECONDS

This great range of pocket city guides will have you in the know in no time. Lightweight and packed with detail on the most important things from shopping and sights to non-stop nightlife, they knock spots off chunkier, clunkier versions. Titles include:

Editorial/project management: Lisa Plumridge
Copy editor: Ismay Atkins
Layout/DTP: Alison Rayner and Pat Hinsley
Proofreader: Wendy Janes

The publishers would like to thank the following individuals and organisations for supplying their copyright photographs for this book: Oscar Ruben Calero de Diago/BigStockPhoto.com, page 127; Laura Frenkel ©iStockphoto.com, page 115; Ercilla Hotels, page 42; Frank Sebastian Hansen ©iStockphoto.com, page 29; Graham Heywood ©iStockphoto.com, pages 7, 52 & 101; Iratxe Ormatza Imatz, pages 25, 32, 38, 70 & 87; Rainer Schmied, page 123; Luis Seco ©iStockphoto.com, page 92; StockExpert.com, pages 119 & 131; Jorge Vicente, page 141; Jarno Gonzalez Zarraonandia ©iStockphoto.com, pages 81 & 134; Neil Setchfield, all other pages.

Send your thoughts to
books@thomascook.com

* **Found a great bar, club, shop or must-see sight that we don't feature?**
* **Like to tip us off about any information that needs a little updating?**
* **Want to tell us what you love about this handy little guidebook and more importantly how we can make it even handier?**

Then here's your chance to tell all! Send us ideas, discoveries and recommendations today and then look out for your valuable input in the next edition of this title.

Email the above address (stating the title) or write to:
CitySpots Project Editor, Thomas Cook Publishing, PO Box 227, Coningsby Road, Peterborough PE3 8SB, UK.